Martha Nussbaum

MARTHA NUSSBAUM

Ancient Philosophy, Civic Education
and Liberal Humanism

Anders Burman & Synne Myrebøe (eds.)

Södertörns högskola

Södertörns högskola
(Södertörn University)
The Library
SE-141 89 Huddinge

www.sh.se/publications

Cover: Jonathan Robson
Cover image: *Eros. Attic red-figure bobbin,*
ca. 470 BC–450 BC, Painter of London D 12. Marie-
Lan Nguyen/Wikimedia Commons (Public Domain)
Graphic form: Per Lindblom & Jonathan Robson

Stockholm 2019

Södertörn Studies in Intellectual and Cultural History 1
Södertörn Academic Studies 77
ISSN 1650-433X
ISBN 978-91-88663-84-9 (print)
ISBN 978-91-88663-85-6 (digital)

Contents

Introduction

Anders Burman and Synne Myrebøe

During her long academic career, Martha Nussbaum has purposefully followed the advice John Rawls once proffered while she was at Harvard: to pull philosophy into the public realm and make it relevant for life.[1] In addition to writing theoretical books, she has consistently sought to bring to bear her theoretical investigations on contemporary ethical and political questions. Often ranked as one of the world's most influential contemporary philosophers, Nussbaum's work impacts on issues as different as same-sex marriage, human rights, the politics of redistribution, global justice as well as college curricula. While practically engaged, her theoretical interventions in all these fields exhibit a solid foundation in the history of philosophy, specifically in Greek and Roman antiquity.

Ever since her doctoral dissertation, *Aristotle's De Motu Animalium*, defended in 1975 and subsequently published in 1978,[2] Aristotle as well as Socrates, Plato, Seneca and other ancient thinkers have remained recurring points of reference in Nussbaum's work. Her academic breakthrough came in 1986 with the publication of *The Fragility of Goodness: Luck and Ethics in Greek Tragedy and Philosophy*, in which she investigates ancient

---

[1] Martha Nussbaum, "Introduction", in *Philosophical Interventions: Reviews, 1986–2011* (Oxford: Oxford University Press, 2012), p. 1.
[2] Martha Nussbaum, *Aristotle's De Motu Animalium: Text with Translation, Commentary, and Interpretive Essays* (Princeton: Princeton University Press, 1978).

conceptions of human vulnerability, moral luck and the good life.[3] Since then a large number of works have followed, foremost among them are *The Therapy of Desire: Theory and Practice in Hellenistic Ethics* (1994), which studies the ethical thought and moral praxis of the ancient schools of the Epicureanism, skepticism and stoicism; *Upheavals of Thought: The Intelligence of Emotions* (2001), which, in analyzing not only philosophers but also literary authors, such as Dante, Emily Bronte, Marcel Proust and James Joyce, investigates the cognitive aspects of emotions or, as Nussbaum puts it, emotional intelligence; and *Political Emotions: Why Love Matters for Justice* (2013), in which she highlights and explores the fundamental importance of love, compassion and other emotions in political life.[4] This is just a selection of her prolific intellectual output. To date, Nussbaum's immense productivity covers more than 470 articles and 25 books, many of which have been translated into other languages.

In line with Nussbaum's comprehensive work, previous research is to be found within a wide range of disciplines.[5] In this

---

[3] Martha Nussbaum, *The Fragility of Goodness: Luck and Ethics in Greek Tragedy and Philosophy* (Cambridge: Cambridge University Press, 1986).

[4] Martha Nussbaum, *The Therapy of Desire: Theory and Practice in Hellenistic Ethics* (Princeton: Princeton University Press, 1994); *Upheavals of Thought: The Intelligence of Emotions* (Cambridge: Cambridge University Press, 2001); *Political Emotions: Why Love Matters for Justice* (Cambridge: Harvard University Press, 2013).

[5] Some of the more extensive studies on Nussbaum's work include the following: Nora Hämäläinen, *A Literary Turn: Rethinking the Roles of Generalization and Theory in Anglo-American Moral Philosophy* (Helsinki: University of Helsinki, Department of Philosophy, 2009); Emma Franchini, *Human Rights and Martha Nussbaum's Capabilities Approach. Connections and Interrelations* (Rom: 1LUISS Guido Carli University, 2012); Johannes Nathschläger, *Der Begriff des guten Lebens bei Martha Nussbaum: Eine kritische Untersuchung des Capabilities Approach* (München: Tectum 2013); Jenny Ehnberg, *Globalization, Justice, and Communication: A Critical Study of Global Ethics* (Uppsala: Uppsala University, 2015); Adam Galamaga, *Philosophie der Menscherechte von Martha C. Nussbaum: Eine Einfurung in den Capabilities Approach* (Marburg: Tectum, 2014); Philipp Hauner, *Das Bildungsideal bei Martha Nussbaum* (München: Grin Verlag, 2014), and Synne Myrebøe, *Kultiveringens politik: Martha Nussbaum, antiken och filosofins*

volume we have gathered scholars mainly from philosophy and intellectual history to discuss Nussbaum's work. The principal foci for this anthology are Nussbaum's treatments of ancient philosophy, civic education and liberal humanism, three areas that are intertwined in her work but less explored in the research on Nussbaum's philosophical oeuvre. The purpose of the volume is to provide a general overview of these three aspects of Nussbaum's thinking as well as to raise some concerns and critical questions at specific parts of her work. Starting with Nussbaum's first published texts from 1972 up to and including her most recent work, the seven interpretations of Nussbaum's thought presented here are organized so as to mirror Nussbaum's own intellectual chronology. In addition to this, the volume is also thematically organized, in so far as the first three articles deal with Nussbaum's readings and uses of ancient thinkers—specifically, Heraclitus, Plato and Aristotle, respectively—while the other texts examine her views on liberal education, cosmopolitanism, human rights and aging.

In "Martha Nussbaum and Heraclitus: Early Notions on Interpretation", Synne Myrebøe turns to Nussbaum's first articles, originally published in 1972 in the journal *Phronesis,* on Heraclitus' concepts of *psyche* and *logos.* Here Nussbaum establishes a notion of interpretation that is further developed in *Fragility of Goodness* and will be of importance for her later philosophical work. In these early articles, Nussbaum reveals a tension between the individual soul and the sense of tradition from which the individual departs. This tension can be seen as paradigmatic for her politics of interpretation. What Myrebøe

praktik ["The Politics of Cultivation: Martha Nussbaum, Antiquity and the Practice of Philosophy"] (Umeå: Umeå University, 2019). See also Ronald L. Hall, *The Human Embrace: The Love of Philosophy and the Philosophy of Love: Kirkegaard, Cavell, Nussbaum* (University Park, PA: Pennsylvania State University Press, 2000); John Deigh, "Nussbaum's Defence of the Stoic Theory of Emotions", *Quarterly Law Review* 19, 2000 and Deigh, "Nussbaum's Account of Compassion", *Philosophy and Phenomenological Research,* Vol. 68, No. 2, 2004.

discerns in Nussbaum's reading of Heraclitus is a defense of pluralistic sensitivity that transgresses conservative readings of the past. From this perspective, interpretations of the past become an ethico-political question for the present.

The next article, "Nussbaum's Platonic Mirror" by Mats Persson, investigates Nussbaum's readings of Plato. Against the background of a discussion surrounding how Nussbaum brings together philological, historical and philosophical perspectives, Persson emphasizes three aspects of her account of Plato. The first coheres around her interpretation of reason in Plato's work; here, Persson problematizes the line of demarcation Nussbaum draws between noetic reason, on the one hand, and desires and emotions, on the other. Thereafter he examines Nussbaum's psychological understanding of the characters populating Plato's dialogues. While Persson does not deny the significant benefits that come with adopting a dramatic approach to the dialogues, as can be found in Nussbaum's *The Fragility of Goodness*, he nonetheless claims that Nussbaum does not sufficiently do justice to the philosophical dimensions of the dialogues. Finally, Persson discusses Nussbaum's view of Plato's philosophical development, in relation to other contemporary interpretations of Plato.

Departing from Nussbaum's reading of Aristotelian epistemology, Charlotta Weigelt raises one of the core objections directed toward Nussbaum, namely Nussbaum's claim that Aristotle represents a radical break with Plato's philosophy of transcendence. The title of the article, "Nussbaum, Aristotle, and the Problem of Anthropocentrism", points to what Weigelt sees as Nussbaum's mission: to develop a contemporary notion of ethics that overcomes the entrenched positions of subjectivism and objectivism. The article investigates how Nussbaum interprets Aristotle's understanding of human nature and how his teleological determinism is translated into a contemporary defense of rational argumentation. However, in Nussbaum's redeployment of Aristotle for a contemporary defense of humanism, the question is whether she does not repeat the very "naturalization of morality" she wants to move beyond. According to Weigelt, a central problem with Nussbaum's understanding of Aristotle is her inability to read Plato as the teacher to whom Aristotle responds.

From the late 1980s, Nussbaum developed her capabilities approach, based on her work on Aristotle. This project was initiated in close collaboration with the Indian Nobel Prize-winning economist Amartya Sen for the United Nations University in Helsinki and the World Institute for Development Economic Research.[6] In contrast to other theories of justice, Nussbaum argues that the capabilities approach focuses on "what people are actually able to do and to be" and treats every human being "as an end and none as a mere tool of the ends of others".[7]

Nussbaum's Aristotelian-inspired capabilities approach is an important background to her educational thinking. She points out that an Aristotelian education, in the form that she maintains, "aims at the cultivation of certain powers of mind" and "realizes that these general powers are developed in many different ways, by many different courses of study."[8] In *Cultivating Humanity: A Classical Defense of Reform in Liberal Education* (1997), Nussbaum highlights what she sees as the desired capabilities with respect to higher education, especially the kind of liberal arts education that strives to promote students' active political life. Considering Nussbaum's Aristotelian orientation, it is unsurprising that she is particularly interested in the tradition of liberal education, for which the study of classical languages and ancient philosophy, literature and culture has always been of primary concern. Similar to other advocates of liberal education, Nussbaum defends the classical heritage, but at the same time she points out that it is necessary to develop this cultural and intellectual heritage. If the inheritance may continue to be a living force it must

---

[6] See Amartya Sen & Martha Nussbaum (eds.), *The Quality of Life* (Oxford: Clarendon Press, 1993).

[7] Martha Nussbaum, *Women and Human Development: The Capabilities Approach* (Cambridge: Cambridge University Press, 2000), p. 5.

[8] Martha Nussbaum, "Aristotelian Social Democracy", in R. Bruce Douglass, Gerald M. Mara & Henry S. Richardson (eds.), *Liberalism and the Good* (New York: Routledge, 1990), p. 236.

change over time and keep apace with societal change. Hence, the institutionalized form of liberal education that Nussbaum defends is one that must be adjusted to our contemporary world.

In "Martha Nussbaum and Liberal Education", Anders Burman explores and contextualizes Nussbaum's views on liberal arts education and educational policy. The main source here is *Cultivating Humanity*, but to some degree also *Not for Profit: Why Democracy Needs the Humanities* (2010). In her vindication of an updated version of liberal education, Nussbaum argues that all higher education, regardless of its professional orientation, should be characterized by a cultivation of three general capacities among students, namely the ability to critically examine one's own prejudices, the empathic capacity to see oneself in others and finally the ability to regard oneself as a world citizen. Burman examines each of these proposals, relating them to their educational, political and philosophical contexts. In our globalized and multicultural world, Nussbaum stresses that it is of the utmost importance for education to be designed in an appropriate way. For her this implies a broad humanistic curriculum. In this way, her defense of a reform of liberal education is at the same time a plea for the humanities and classical studies.

Sharon Rider further deepens the depiction of Nussbaum's philosophy of education. In "Cosmopolitanism Begins at Home: Or, On Knowing One's Place", Rider focuses on ideas of world citizenship and critical thinking and how they are elaborated in *Cultivating Humanity*. Instead of linking Nussbaum's conception of human cultivation with the classical tradition, as Burman and most other Nussbaum scholars tend to do, Rider puts emphasis on the importance of Immanuel Kant's for Nussbaum's democratic educational ideal. From Kant's exposition of the human capacity to reason, particularly his three maxims in *Critique of Judgment*—that you should think for yourself, put yourself in the place of others, and always think consistently—as well as his insistence that such thinking requires education, Rider draws out a set of similarities between Kant's and Nussbaum's argumentation. However, unlike Kant, Nussbaum stresses that this cultivation of the mind must be supplemented by an education of people's hearts and emotions. Although this seems to be justified and valuable, Rider draws attention to some short-comings in Nussbaum's way of conceptualizing thinking, which in part is due to how she holds onto a rather limited understanding of the rational, dignified life.

Jenny Ehnberg's article, "Capabilities and Human Dignity: On Martha Nussbaum's Understanding of Justice and Human Rights", departs from Nussbaum's work on the capabilities approach in *Women and Human Development* (1999). This book sets out to consider the universal status of the list of capabilities, with focus on the lived conditions of Indian women. However, Ehnberg notes that the voices of these women are scarcely discernible behind Nussbaum's own. Although Nussbaum has emphasized that her list of basic capabilities should be revisable, Ehnberg points out that the list now has remained the same for over two decades. Scrutinizing the capabilities approach as a model for justice, Ehnberg argues that Nussbaum's ideas of capabilities as a measure for human dignity can be understood as sufficientarianism and thus ends up legitimizing inequalities. As a theory of justice, Ehnberg finds it plausible that Nussbaum formulates justice in terms of development. However, she argues that her list of capabilities is deficient and in need of further development.

Finally, in the last article in this volume, "Work, Aging and Justice", Nora Hämäläinen discusses Nussbaum's critique of compulsory retirement in Finland. With her book *Aging Thoughtfully*, written in cooperation with Saul Levermore, Nussbaum engages in a current debate about the challenges associated with an aging population. While generally affirming the Scandinavian welfare-model, Nussbaum directs a harsh critique toward compulsory retirement, referring to it as "one of the great moral evils of our times". The fact that the state supports retirement at a certain age is, for Nussbaum, based on prejudices about the capabilities of elderly citizens. Instead, she defends the individual right to choose the appropriate time for one's own retirement as well as a reduction of work-related goods such as assistants and office-space. For Hämäläinen, this argument is based on Nussbaum's personal experiences and thus represents a regression from her overall views on political and economic redistribution. Another problem that Hämäläinen raises is that Nussbaum seems to be ignorant of many contemporary discussions on life and work and that her thoughts on aging and justice risk reproducing social and economic hierarchies in favor of maintaining conditions under current capitalist societies. Rather than simply supporting secure privileged positions, Hämäläinen calls for a new social imagery in which meaningful activities for all ages could be found outside the sphere of paid work.

Throughout her academic work, Nussbaum shows in what ways philosophy is relevant for contemporary political and ethical concerns. Even though this covers some of the main threads in Nussbaum's authorship, this anthology provides only a glance at her vast philosophical work. However, we hope that the following articles, which critically engage with Nussbaum's thought, will spark further interest in her work, generally speaking, as well as more specifically garner more attention with respect to how contemporary discussions on ancient philosophy relate to some of the most pressing political and ethical issues of our time.

Martha Nussbaum and Heraclitus: Early Notions on Interpretation

Synne Myrebøe

If we know what we ought to do, why do we not just do it? In ancient Greek philosophy, this was the troublesome question of *akrasia,* or lack of will. For Socrates, *akrasia* simply meant ignorance; as long as you do not practice what you teach, you have not really understood what you are teaching. Socrates' dismissal of Athenian tragedy as offering pedagogical and therapeutic lessons on human failure, make plain from the outset his endeavor to overcome the human condition in which the void between theory and praxis seems impassable. Through the art of reason and the taming of the passions, Socrates faces death unruffled.

Although Socrates is one of Martha Nussbaum's paragons, she rejects the idea that philosophy is a way of preparing for death. In her extensive work on ethical and political philosophy, she argues that the pervading influence of Platonic anti-tragedy must be transgressed in order to establish stability within contemporary politics. The problem of *akrasia* is not in the lack of knowing, as Nussbaum sees it, but rather uncultivated sentiments. Throughout her work, she returns to the classical question of how to live, stressing how this must be a leading question in all human activities. Since the mid-nineties, she has related this question to a number of topics from literature to law and politics. She recalls the Aristotelian notion of a cultivation of a second nature whereby "we can learn to feel appropriately, just as we can learn to act appropriately".[1] The art of cultivation is nothing less than a thoroughgoing transformation of the self, what Nussbaum in her late work characterizes as a transition from un-reflected prejudices to a self-scrutinized way of living. To those who work hard to change their bad habits, Nussbaum suggests that the problem of *akrasia* might be dissolved without losing touch with matter.

The fact that Nussbaum presents the Aristotelian art of cultivation as radically different from Plato's philosophical approach might be considered as a rhetorical framing of her own project. Actualizing the Ancient Greek tradition where different philosophical schools offered to teach their students a certain view of the world, Nussbaum develops her own understanding of philosophy as a way of life in which cultivation is considered as a way of practicing theory, namely as a way of learning to see. What view then, or vision, does Nussbaum's philosophical schooling offer?

For Nussbaum, contemporary crises in law, higher education and in politics, can be understood as arising from a general ignorance about how senses and emotions direct people's perception and understanding about the world. She insists that historical as well as contemporary political philosophy have ignored the role of emotions for an unquestioned acceptance of rational choice theories. In response Nussbaum calls for a masscultivation of political emotions.[2] To some this may sound illiberal, but Nussbaum will contend that all societies cultivate emotions, and out of necessity. She argues that a vast part of the the history of Western philosophy has struggled to cultivate an ignorance of emotions. For this reason, the lessons of Greek tragedies, which Socrates himself rejected, constitute a leitmotiv for the entirety of her philosophical work. When in *Love's Knowledge* (1992) she

[1] Martha Nussbaum, *Political Emotions: Why Love Matters for Justice* (Cambridge: Harvard University Press, 2013), p. 65.
[2] Martha Nussbaum, *Anger and Forgiveness: Resentment, Generosity, Justice* (New York: Oxford University Press, 2016), p. 218.

recalls her own education, we are presented with an early passion for tragedy:

> I was finding in the Greek tragic poets a recognition of the ethical importance of contingency, a deep sense of the problem of conflicting obligations, and a recognition of the ethical importance of the passions, that I found more rarely, if at all, in the admitted philosophers, whether ancient or modern.[3]

What the authors of tragedy made it possible for Nussbaum to effectively index was some basic ethical and philosophical questions surrounding conditions of life and on how to live. But the young Nussbaum's expectations on higher education as a continuous path of scrutinizing existential and ethical wonderings turned out to be a challenge; the intellectual cultures at New York and Harvard University seemed uninterested in fostering the institutional conditions under which dialogues between literature, ethics and philosophy could take place. Nussbaum ended up in the Classics department, where she wrote her dissertation on Aristotle's *De Motu Animalium*.[4] In her translation of Aristotle's text as well as in the following five interpretative essays, Nussbaum criticizes the disciplinary order between which she finds herself split. She had, in fact, already presented this critical notion on contemporary disciplinarity in her first two articles, "ΨYXH in Heraclitus, I" and "ΨYXH in Heraclitus, II", both articles published in the journal *Phronesis* in 1972, where she discusses the concept of *psyche* and *logos* in Heraclitus.[5]

Now, why does Nussbaum direct her attention to Heraclitus? His poetic notions were considered obscure already among his

---

[3] Martha Nussbaum, *Love's Knowledge: Essays on Philosophy and Literature* (New York: Oxford University Press, 1990), p. 14.

[4] Martha Nussbaum, *Aristotle's De Motu Animalium: Text with Translation, Commentary, and Interpretive Essays* (Princeton: Princeton University Press, 1978).

[5] Martha Nussbaum, "ΨYXH in Heraclitus, I" and "ΨYXH in Heraclitus, II", both articles in *Phronesis*, 1 January 1972, Vol. 1.

own contemporaries, and the authenticity of his fragments have been questioned within the history of philosophy, since their remnants have been preserved only on account of later interpretations. A large part of the Heraclitian fragments were collected by Friedrich Schleiermacher in 1807, and for the philosophical direction later formulated by Marx, Nietzsche, and Freud, the dialectics of Heraclitus was an essential key to a world of concealment. With the exception of her references to Kant, Nussbaum rarely touched upon the heritage of German idealism. Nonetheless, it is precisely through her reading of Heraclitus that we can trace in what way Nussbaum offers her own critical commentary to the rationalistic path of the Enlightenment, which came to feature within Anglo-American epistemological debates during the 20th century.

The international reception of Nussbaum's work has showed little, if any interest in these early texts. In this article, I argue that Nussbaum's interpretation on Heraclitus is indispensable for an understanding of her philosophical work and the art of reading she proposes. In what follows I will suggest that her interpretive reading of Heraclitus offers a more radical notion of praxis than what otherwise appears in her philosophical oeuvre. To this end, I will draw attention to three aspects of Nussbaum's reading of Heraclitus. The first aspect considers Heraclitus' philosophy as a break with the Homeric tradition. The second will show how Nussbaum interprets Heraclitus to be the first psychologist. Finally, the third aspect will reveal in what way her reading of Heraclitus touches on questions surrounding her own methodological approach further developed in subsequent works, and how precisely this approach relates to her specific ideas regarding cultivation and self-transformation.

Breaking up with Homer

One of Heraclitus' more famous notions is what Plato described as *panta rei*, that everything flows. The transience of water is a recurrent theme in Heraclitus, for example in fragment 36:

For souls it is death to become water, for water it is death to become earth; out of earth water comes-to-be, and out of water soul.[6]

The consideration that the soul is mortal is, Nussbaum writes, unthinkable among Heraclitus' contemporaries. When *psyche* is mentioned in the pre-Socratic literature, it is always as an immortal substance. In the Homeric narrative, the soul is what takes leave of the body once one's last breath has been taken. The eternal life of the soul entails that ideas remain as shadows of the past, wherefrom they can be recalled, traced or understood as a given—albeit hidden or unnoticed—treasure.

Hence with Heraclitus, Nussbaum sees a rupture in this image of cyclical and reproductive time where he introduces a new temporality. Contrary to Homer, Heraclitus considers the past to be part of a constantly productive understanding. One could say that the past is in the present, just as the present is born by the past. In this way, Heraclitus' philosophical approach makes an interpretive connection between past and future and between the individuals and the community consisting of the living as well as the dead and unborn. The explicit critique of the Homeric tradition, which appears in Heraclitus' fragments, corresponds to a problem Nussbaum recognizes in contemporary ethical and political debates. Her aim is to formulate philosophy as a way of life, according to which the history of philosophy is not understood as ruins from the past, but as a potential resource for contemporary thought and for the effectuation of social change in the present. Thus, just like Heraclitus, the task to which Nussbaum returns is the risk of trusting appearances without considering their inseparable hidden parts.[7]

---

[6] Heraclitus, *The Cosmic Fragments, ed. G. S. Kirk* (Cambridge, 1954), fragment 36, p. 339.

[7] As Nussbaum sees prejudices as part of the unconscious, she is critical to the literary and philosophical theory of ordinary language philosophy, which she claims is too close to utilitarianism. Martha Nussbaum, *The Therapy of Desire*, p. 25 and p. 33.

Unlike the nostalgic conservatism characteristic of some of her neo-Aristotelian peers, Nussbaum stresses an ambition to combine Aristotelian ethics with ideas of Enlightenment. From this perspective, her reading of Heraclitus can be seen as a critical note on how the heritage of Enlightenment has evolved within the Anglo-American tradition. In situating the notion of psyche within an immanent ontology, Nussbaum seeks to re-negotiate the very dualisms between matter and soul, emotions and reason, literature and philosophy.

Within the European philosophical tradition, epistemology, ethics and aesthetics are constituent parts of political philosophy. Hence, a pertinent question is why, with her autobiographical note of disciplinary alienation as well as her concerns for both literature and politics, Nussbaum nonetheless remains evasive with respect to her own connection with the development of the German philosophical tradition during the 19th and 20th centuries and its contemporary work on Ancient philosophy. Thus, as Seyla Benhabib writes, Nussbaum's philosophy can be characterized as a branch of neo-Aristotelianism that dovetails with certain ethico-political issues discussed by Hans-Georg Gadamer.[8] An active dialogue with Gadamer and his critique of positivism, as well as, in particular, Gadamer's specific works on Heraclitus, could have offered an alternative to the analytical tradition by which Nussbaum finds herself marginalized. Yet, although many of Nussbaum's questions are discussed within the so-called continental philosophical tradition, the critical and hermeneutic traditions remain conspicuously absent in her work, with the exception of some comments. It is relevant to ask why this may be? Perhaps the absence of these conversations can be understood against the background of a general skepticism in the United States toward the German tradition during the decades after Word War II, parallel to the political positioning of

---

[8] Seyla Benhabib, *Situating the Self: Gender, Community and Postmodernism in Contemporary Ethics* (Cambridge: Polity, 1992), p. 49.

the cold war. Whether, however, this serves as an adequate explanation regarding her neglect of Heidegger and Gadamer remains unclear. What is interesting is how, through her interpretation of psyche as a center for cognition, Nussbaum presents a psychologically oriented philosophy outside the continental tradition as well as outside contemporary catholic Aristotelianism.

Through Heraclitus' interpretation of psyche as a cognitive and linguistic faculty that remains for every individual unique, Nussbaum argues that he opened up the very possibility for a radically new understanding of knowledge, pointing toward the philosophical dawn of 4th century BC.

Heraclitus as the First Psychologist

Although Nussbaum was to present her theory of cognitive emotions, according to which emotions are described as rational judgments of value much later, the outline of the theory can nonetheless be discerned in her reading of Heraclitus. The spider-simile in fragment 67a, a key figure in Nussbaum's reading of Heraclitus as the first psychologist, serves also as the paragon for her ethical approach and interpretive work:

> As a spider [...] standing in the middle of its web is aware the instant a fly breaks any one of its threads and runs there swiftly as though lamenting the breaking of the thread; so a man's soul when any part of his body is hurt hastily goes there as though intolerant of the hurt to a body to which it is strongly and harmoniously conjoined.[9]

This fragment, which derives from a 12th century text discussing Plato's *Timaeus*, remains one of the most disputed fragments, and yet it is central to Nussbaum's reading. The emphasis that Heraclitus places on the soul as a central cognitive faculty is a point developed further in her dissertation on Aristotle where

---

[9] Hans Ruin, comment to fragment 67a in Herakleitos, *Fragment* (Lund: Propexus, 1997), p. 150.

this faculty, or organ, is seen as a simile for the heart as well as for the city. I will not advance any further with this political metaphor here. What is important is the notion of a cognitive potential that has to be cultivated in order for its possibilities to be developed.

Nussbaum's psychological approach should not be confused with a contemporary understanding of psychology, now recognized as a discipline within the social sciences. In Plato as well as in Aristotle, we find expositions on the soul according to which politics cultivates the citizens of *polis*. Like these ancient philosophers, Nussbaum argues that a rigorous knowledge of *psyche* as a cognitive faculty must be the ground on which political decisions rest. In harnessing the spider-simile as part of her own methodological approach, a specific interpretation becomes existentially constitutive for both an individual as well as for the community in which the person takes part. Body and thought, senses and perception, are indivisible in any given interpretation of, and action that take place in, the world. What Nussbaum sees as the lessons of tragedy is the capability to act according to a practical knowledge, which is conditioned by a volatile understanding of human need and the fragility of goodness.

Nussbaum describes how the Heraclitian spider, *psyche,* is "self-moving and capable of directing its movement", but it constitutes no capability in and by itself. Hence, in the same way that the spider moves over its net, connecting its different parts, *psyche* creates the conditions for human understanding, combining language with experience.[10] Understood in this way, Heraclitus' critique of Homer is directed toward the idea of the latter whereupon knowledge is considered as the capability to speak your mother-tongue and repeat, or reproduce, what is already taught. Instead, Nussbaum's Heraclitus insists on the necessity to cultivate one's *psyche* as a faculty to understand. Knowledge, *logos*, or what there is to understand, is the object

[10] Nussbaum, "ΨΥΧΗ in Heraclitus, I", p. 8.

for an interpretive understanding that is created by the web of *psyche*. What Heraclitus might have been the first to understand, at least according to Nussbaum, was what we could call a "cognitive capacity"; learning is not a passive reception through the senses. Only through interpretive acts does understanding take place. The act of reading thus changes what is read, as well as the one who reads. Hence, like the reader, the text does not remain constant; the river we step into is never the same.

The approach to the philosophical tradition that appears in Nussbaum's reading of Heraclitus reflects her own practice of philosophy along with her later ideas on the fragility of goodness.[11] Thus, as Plato feared, the insight of Heraclitus has risky consequences. Relating to Heraclitus' classic predication that everything flows, Nussbaum writes:

> Although there is no stable constituent in a river – though the waters are always different – yet there is a sense in which the river is the same. Its identity does not depend on the preservation of the same waters. [...] As a man's fame is handed down from generation to generations among mortals, it is constantly reinterpreted and re-expressed; it is never, in fact, the same. And yet, as the fame of one man, it is the same, and the changing continuity of human tradition does not destroy its identity. For example, not two people, throughout the centuries, have given the same account of [...] Heraclitus.[12]

What will remain is up to the living, not the dead, she writes. Hence the past cannot be understood from another perspective other than as it reveals itself in a present reading. I suggest that Nussbaum's attention to Heraclitus' ideas on the soul should be regarded as a defense of an actualizing art of reading, a reading that withdraws from the act of seeking the truth in a given past. Although Heraclitus insists that the truth loves to hide itself,

[11] Martha Nussbaum, *The Fragility of Goodness: Luck and Ethics in Greek Tragedy and philosophy* (1986).
[12] Nussbaum, "Heraclitus II", p. 162.

Nussbaum writes that his dialectical insight does not mean that he countenances a withdrawal from ethical judgments:

> We must understand the relativity of relative terms. [---] Ethical judgements are relative, but they must be made; and the recognition of the relative nature of our ethical terms should not trick us into believing they are meaningless.[13]

To be able to make good judgments, Nussbaum insists on the necessity to cultivate perception and emotions. And just as Heraclitus highlights *psyche* as a particular human faculty, he also emphasizes the different temptations with which human beings are confronted. His understanding of *psyche* and its potential for self-awareness implies, as Nussbaum sees it, the possibility for the individual to transcend the immediate pleasures of prejudices and take responsibility for its own life.[14]

Heraclitus writes that a dry soul has self-control, whereas a watery soul lacks the same; sleep and drunkenness are taken as examples of watery conditions.[15] In the Greek tradition, to abandon oneself to wet conditions are the similes for death. However, Nussbaum emphasizes that Heraclitus distances himself from any such ascetic restrains: getting drunk and the need to sleep are, he insists, inseparable parts of the human condition. The message that Nussbaum wants to put forward is rather the importance of self-knowledge as a constant endeavor.[16] Recognizing human beings as neither gods nor animals brings up the ethical question on how to live, it also shows up the human life as a political life, another recurring theme in Nussbaum's Aristotelian writings. Heraclitus' thoughts on the mortal soul indicate for Nussbaum that the human condition and the transcendence

---

[13] Nussbaum, "Heraclitus II", p. 165.
[14] Nussbaum, "Heraclitus II", p. 159.
[15] Nussbaum's comments on Heraclitus' fragments 36, 77 and 117 in Nussbaum, "Heraclitus II", pp. 153, 159.
[16] Nussbaum's comments on Heraclitus' fragment 116 in Nussbaum, "Heraclitus II", p. 159.

of the soul are re-thought. To make reincarnation or past-mortal fame as incitement for virtuous action, as was the view of Homer, is here replaced with an idea of the particular life as having intrinsic value for both the mortal *psyche* and the immortal *logos*. Here, the Delphic call to "Know thyself" is presented as a meditative exercise led by the individual, where one scrutinizes and examines *logos* from a unique perspective. Thus, the contemplative practice in Nussbaum's theory is first of all an activity, a potentiality actualized in matter. What Heraclitus does is to bear in mind contemporary and traditional ideas while changing the meaning of their content. Maybe this can give us a hint of the methodological protocols that Nussbaum herself develops and follows?

Philosophy or Barbarism: Exercising the Art of Interpretation

As we have seen in Nussbaum's actualization of the spider-simile, capabilities for ethical action requires that one is inducted into a way of living that fosters perspectival pluralism and a sensitive understanding. Without proper learning, your senses and your language will deceive you, Nussbaum writes. Or as Heraclitus puts it: "Eyes and ears are bad witnesses to men who have barbarian souls."[17]

Now, Nussbaum argues that in Heraclitus' time *barbarian* solely meant someone who does not speak Greek. Thus being a barbarian only meant that you need education to cultivate what Aristotle later called the second nature. An important aspect here is that Nussbaum rejects the later interpretation of Aristotle's *telos* as a determinate understanding. Rather, what we consider to be the right way to live and to be is always the focus for a deliberative discussion, or for reaching an overlapping consensus, as Nussbaum says referring to John Rawls. Hence, what is recognized as either civilized or barbaric varies across different times and places. But in order to have this discussion on how to

---

[17] Heraclitus, fragment 107, cited in Nussbaum, "Heraclitus I", p. 9.

live, we must first learn to direct our love from our own needs toward a heterogeneous common good. Also, and this is at the core of Heraclitian dialectics, humans need to understand the secret of nature as loving to hide itself. Every word carries its own negation; day means nothing without night, justice nothing without injustice etc. Heraclitus' lesson seems to be that the world is not just exposed out there for humans to explore through their senses. Understanding also requires a connecting and interpreting faculty that makes sense of the senses. How language is understood is thus key to a wider understanding of the world. The importance of cultivating the sense of the senses is apparent in Nussbaum's interpretation of fragment 34. The fragment reads:

> People, who fail to make connections, when they hear, seem like deaf people. What they say bear witness that although they are present, they are absent.[18]

What Nussbaum emphasizes here is speech, and its connection with a capability to listen and interpret. As long as a person has not understood what he says, he is still a barbarian, that is to say, a stranger to what is said and even to his own speech. What appears for thought and perception are not phenomena that expose themselves in their own right, rather they are the result of a perceptive capacity. While, in these early texts on Heraclitus, Nussbaum has a thin understanding of language—something she will develop later—what is central here is her understanding of *psyche* as an active, connecting organ and interpretive faculty. At the same time, she interprets *logos* as an ever-changing and indefinite object of knowledge, from which the conditions for understanding (*nous*) are created.[19] If *psyche* so to say rises out of *logos* then at the same time *psyche* explores and creates *logos*, with every resultant and new interpretation expanding and changing what can be explored.

---

[18] Heraclitus, fragment 34, cited in Nussbaum, "Heraclitus I", p. 12.
[19] Nussbaum, "Heraclitus I", p. 14.

At the end of her second article on Heraclitus, Nussbaum describes his inventive understanding of the soul as both a beginning and a goal for a single individual, understood as a knowledge producing and, performing, subject. This understanding has radical consequences for how we might conceive the limits of knowledge:

> He emphasizes the capacity of each man for self-seeking and self-knowledge, and teaches the importance of self-restraint. [...] Man's potential for self-development in terms of ψυχή [*psyche*] is unlimited; and understanding leads to new understanding.[20]

Nussbaum finds significant in Heraclitus the idea that *psyche* works in the individual life both as something unique and particular. Hence, language for Heraclitus is nothing that is traded directly from one generation to another. It is, in fact, never the same. In contrast to Homer's thoughts on the eternal life of souls in Hades, Nussbaum considers Heraclitus as developing an immanent art of interpretation according to which cognition constitutes the single person's relation to the world. Departing from Heraclitus' understanding of the soul, Nussbaum discerns in human experience a connecting tissue between language and thought, both with respect to individuals as well as in terms of a shared humanity.[21] Life and death, like night and day, are latent in the dialectics of Heraclitian thought, and equally so in the idea that there is "unity in difference—difference in unity".[22]

An overarching goal of all education must, according to Nussbaum, be to transcend the field of immediate experience and to strive toward a common sensibility, or a sense of a com-

---

[20] Nussbaum, "Heraclitus II", s. 169.
[21] Nussbaum, "Heraclitus I", p. 5.
[22] Hans Ruin, "Unity in Difference – Difference in Unity: Heraclitus and the Truth of Hermeneutics", in Hans Ruin & Nicholas Smith (eds.), *Hermeneutik och tradition: Gadamer och den grekiska filosofin* (Huddinge: Södertörns högskola, 2014), pp. 19-52.

mon world. Conscious of one's own barbaric inclinations—that is, to see from the already seen and to hear according to the already heard—the cultivation of a capacity making possible complex perception must be nurtured in education in order to avoid being misled by prejudices. In the act of transcendence, Nussbaum recognizes a double risk: first, a risk of turning inwards and second an uncritical belief that one has grasped it all. To protect oneself from these risks, Nussbaum defends a dialectical transformation that mimics the existential human condition. In Heraclitus' prophesies, she understands the death of the gods as signaling their irrelevance regarding judgments about human life. Ethical judgments are, as Nussbaum will write many years later, of personal concern and they must depart from the principle of reciprocity between humans.[23] Hence as a reciprocal possibility, common sense is always a radical, thus fragile, potential.

Expecting the Unexpected as an Ethical Condition

Now, what is it that makes Heraclitus such an important thinker for Nussbaum? First of all, we have seen how his understanding of *psyche* provides an entry into philosophy as a way of living, which in itself presents a break with the mythological tradition of Homer, according to which reproduction is the central praxis. In the ancient understanding of humans, in which human beings are placed between the animals and the gods, between mortality and eternity, Nussbaum considers Heraclitus to be the first to elevate human history and language as objects for cognitive understanding. In his thoughts on how the soul of a single individual affects how the world appears for that individual Nussbaum recognizes a gesturing toward the birth of the individual, something that Aristotle will formulate in his own reading of Heraclitus. The main argument that Nussbaum develops here is the risk of being seduced by single measurements of value and knowledge.

---

[23] Martha Nussbaum, "Foreword", in Iris Marion Young, *Responsibility for Justice* (New York: Oxford University Press, 2013).

With his interpretation of *psyche*, Heraclitus also initiates a critique of the traditional view about the afterlife. The fact that later translators have argued that Heraclitus kept his religious convictions on immortality are, for Nussbaum, rather proof of the predominance of Christian interpretation where translations of ancient texts were made to conform to the values of Christendom.[24] For Nussbaum, what these translators omit is the radical potential that Heraclitus represents. In her own reading of ancient philosophy, specifically, in her treatment of how the ancients grappled with ethical, political and epistemological issues, Nussbaum takes as her point of departure precisely this significant potential found in Heraclitus.

As an answer to what is left after death, Nussbaum says, "Nothing' is the most likely solution for Heraclitus' cryptic riddle".[25] But what are the possibilities of a "nothing"? In Nussbaum's reading of Heraclitus, "nothing" is what calls for and serves as an opening for ethics. She points out that ethical questions are irrelevant for the gods, likewise the notion of moral virtues. To be brave or good, Nussbaum argues, is not a question for those who have nothing to lose. Recognizing Heraclitus' thoughts on the unconditional contradiction that follows every concept is what Nussbaum considers as a necessary approach in understanding the complexity of how the world is perceived. In the spider-simile, she emphasizes sensitivity between thinking and what is thought, a reciprocal sensitivity that joins perception and the perceived.

Nussbaum's early articles on Heraclitus show reading to be an individual act, for which no interpretation is alike. Since the past can only be understood from the perspectives taken by a present reading, what remains to be noticed rests on the responsibility of the living, not the dead. Nussbaum urges us to let the text appear through an act of reading, and understands this to be

---

[24] Nussbaum, "Heraclitus II", p. 158.
[25] Nussbaum, "Heraclitus II", p. 158.

a condition for thought. Her claim finds sustenance in Heraclitus' fragment 18:

> If you do not expect the unexpected, you will not find it;
>
> for it is hard to be sought out and difficult.[26]

In the unexpected, we can seize the philosophical wondering as a condition for true knowledge. Here, in Nussbaum's first published articles, we can see the beginning of a broad, epistemological critique. Far from being empirical fragments available for immediate observation, the study of the past is considered as shaping the past as such. The inseparable relation between knowledge and the subject of knowledge in Nussbaum's approach does not resolve itself into relativism. What she sees in this approach is a basic argument on how the history of philosophy implies ethical and individual responsibility. The politics of cultivation, how to let the past appear in the present, is here presented as an ethical question on point of fact that history, and the history of philosophy, is a narrative that we create and are created by.

In Nussbaum's reading of Heraclitus, we can see the contours of her extensive thoughts on cultivation as a quest for ethico-political engagement. Her ideas on cultivation relate to the Ancient Greek and Roman tradition, but at the same time she helps to give new interpretive shape to Ancient philosophy. What appears in this art of reading is an interpretation of the past in which its actuality appears in a changing now. For Aristotle, the difference between memory and recollection was that the latter presupposed a creative mind. The radical potential in Nussbaum's actualizing art of reading, grounded in her early interpretation of Heraclitus, is embedded in the dialectical relation between a repetition of the past and the unraveling of the same in order to create new meaning. This repetitive and at the same time un-

---

[26] Heraclitus, *The Cosmic Fragments*, Fragment 18, p. 231. The Greek word *aporon*, here translated as "difficult", can also be understood as "impassable".

raveling motion characterizes Nussbaum's philosophical work. In her reading of Heraclitus, she criticizes the conservative view on knowledge represented by Homer for the benefit of a more sensitive and pluralistic art of reading which she defends from psychological, ethical and linguistic perspectives. What makes her attempt at widening the number of voices participating in contemporary discussions distinctive is none other than her way of mobilizing the past. Here, the target of Heraclitus' critique can just as well be the positivist tradition that, prior to Nussbaum's own entry into higher education, had contributed significantly to the split between philosophy and literature.

This way of presenting a critique, which is both timeless and bound to particular temporal and spatial contexts, is further developed in Nussbaum's *oeuvre*. But despite her sustained and inventive praxis of exploring ethical, aesthetic and political aspects of education through what it is possible to hear, say and see in certain times and places, she stops short from this constituting a wholesale critique.

Tragedy and politics

Nussbaum's difficulties in finding an intellectual home may be regarded as one reason why her work is hard to define. Is it philosophy? Ethics? Literary work? Political theory? Although she insists that she left Aristotelianism behind in the mid-nineties to the advantage of a political theory inspired by Kant, Marx and Rawls,[27] I claim that a certain cognizance of her reading of ancient philosophy is important in understanding her later work. In her early study of Heraclitus we find the origins of her art of interpretation. Nussbaum's understanding of the inseparable relation between the particular in every single soul or *psyche*, and *logos* as a constantly changing, common and universal heritage, is at the

---

[27] Nussbaum, "Response to papers", *International Journal of Social Economics*, vol. 40, 2013, p. 664.

core of her ideas on cultivation as an individual as well as a political quest.

What we have seen is also how Nussbaum has given a particularly modern interpretation of Heraclitus, which makes him relevant as a contemporary interlocutor in discussions on how to re-think the relations between the past, present and future. Through an actualization of the Heraclitian concepts *psyche* and *logos,* Nussbaum transgresses what she sees as an insufficient understanding of reason with a psychological philosophy. What this amounts to is a particular mode of philosophy that seeks to cultivate a way for humans to live within a tragic cosmic order. When much later she presents her emotional theory in *Upheavals of Thought*, the cultivation of *psyche* is replaced with a cultivation of capabilities, what Aristotle promoted as an actualization of potentials.[28] In *Political Emotions* she argues for a cultivation of political love.

The subject of knowledge, *psyche*, moves and creates its web of knowledge led by its sensitivity towards the particulars. The etymological meaning of truth, *aletheia*, is "to uncover" or "not forget". What Heraclitus reminds us when he says that nature loves to hide itself, is that our senses can deceive us owing to our prejudices. Thus, Nussbaum writes, philosophy takes its start when we discover that the world might be different than what it seems to be. But is the ethical stance of wondering, which Nussbaum defends, a matter of radical displacement?

What Nussbaum's reading of Heraclitus emphasizes is the opening that his philosophy affords, an opening toward a form of interpretation that exists between the past and the future, and for which his significant notions on unity and difference serve as a challenge to the established philosophical tradition. For what is absent will hereafter be seen as present in its absence, and also as a condition for what appears. That Nussbaum emphasizes emo-

[28] Martha Nussbaum, *Upheavals of Thought: The Intelligence of Emotions* (Cambridge: Cambridge University Press, 2001).

tions and body as matter for reason can be seen as an attempt to make what has been ignored visible. However, a problem often raised by her critics is that her arguments on cultivation have a significantly normative, namely already expected, notion of the good that keep up an ignorance for difference. Hence, it is with the goal of becoming capable citizens in a democracy defined by political liberalism that Nussbaum creates her ideas on cultivation.

Tragedy, as Socrates saw it, was the inability of letting go of yourself. His dialectical art did not strive for a quantity of perspectives, but rather the capability to expose oneself for what must be considered a radical fragility: the position of *atopos,* displacement and not knowing. Thus, as the story tells us, Heraclitus left his fragments to the public and went out to the country to live in solitude. Socrates did what he ought to when he rejected to leave Athens and emptied the poison cup. Actualized as Nussbaum's contemporary they are both placed in the middle of an intrusive public discussion on how to live and how to deliberate on the politics of cultivation.

Making yourself vulnerable is not a virtue for Nussbaum. Rather, she searches for the acceptance of the fragility of life as that over which we have no control. As a rhetorical grip, aiming at expanding and reforming institutions, Nussbaum's political approach makes sense; after all, we can see her position informing her extensive dialogues with law, higher education and human rights. A relevant comparison of her Heraclitian spider-simile is the voyagers of the Grand Tour tradition, and its important influence on the liberal humanist tradition developed during early modernity. As we know, the spider, as well as the Faustian traveller, is unconditionally captured in its own net, pushed by its own affects and desires.

However, being stuck in tragedy is for Nussbaum the very definition of the human condition. Her emphasis on transition rather than transcendence means that the task of cultivation is not a turning away from the world, but rather as a possibility or potentiality of dwelling in the strange void between theory and praxis, the *atopos* that at one and the same time separates us from ourselves as from each other, just as it is a prerequisite for reciprocity. Thus, the paradigmatic example of Socrates and his true knowledge is, in Nussbaum's interpretation, not only impossible, but also undesirable. For Nussbaum, tragedy as the fragility of goodness is nothing to overcome. On the contrary, it signifies the continuous struggle through which a common world is actualizable, over and over again.

Nussbaum's Platonic Mirror

Mats Persson

Martha Nussbaum often returns to Plato. He is a recurring point of reference, and his philosophy plays an important role in her own philosophical undertakings. Her usage is often emblematic, with Plato signifying an intellectual and ethical position.[1] This kind of praxis is very common when philosophers deal with their past masters, but in Nussbaum's case, there is also a more scholarly aspect. In her early *The Fragility of Goodness: Luck and Ethics in Greek Tragedy and Philosophy* (1986), we find an extensive study of some of Plato's most important dialogues.[2] The results of these investigations lay the foundation for her later more emblematic usage of Plato, and for this reason the focus here will be on Nussbaum's early study.

Given the "industrial" character of Plato-research, it is notable how often one finds references to, and discussions of, Nussbaum's readings. While many of these are positive, her interpretations of Plato have also garnered criticisms. The extent of the attention she has received is probably due in part to her pro-

---

[1] For examples, see Martha Nussbaum, *Love's Knowledge: Essays on Philosophy and Literature* (New York: Oxford University Press, 1990), and Martha Nussbaum, *Upheavals of Thought: The Intelligence of Emotions* (Cambridge: Cambridge University Press, 2001).

[2] Martha Nussbaum, *The Fragility of Goodness: Luck and Ethics in Greek Tragedy and Philosophy* (Cambridge: Cambridge University Press, 1986), pp. 85-233.

minent position in the contemporary debate in and about the humanities, but her far-reaching and at times daring interpretations have also played a role. She has a dual approach to Plato, combining on the one hand philological and historical scholarship with, on the other, a concern for his particular relevance for our own time (i.e. issues and themes in Plato worth knowing today). Although both dimensions are often present in most serious research, at least implicitly, there is also a potential tension between them. Indeed, this seems to be the case in Nussbaum's analysis of the Platonic dialogues.

The basic scholarly aspect is, on the whole, satisfactory. Nussbaum is knowledgeable both with regard to Plato's texts and their ancient contexts, and she engages with contemporary scholarship. The approach is also in line with a couple of recent trends. Nussbaum was an early proponent of so-called "dramatic readings" of the Platonic dialogues, in which the literary form of the texts is treated as philosophically significant. The dramatic design of Plato's dialogues frames the philosophical discussions, and thus provides a necessary context for any interpretation of the content.[3] Furthermore, Nussbaum's readings are at the forefront of contemporary scholarship when it comes to interpreting Plato's texts as a philosophy of life. The dialogues do not thus only present theories, but they portray and propagate a way of life too.[4]

The focus on philosophical relevance can be found throughout *The Fragility of Goodness*. Both orientation and perspective are announced already in the title. The purpose is stated thus: "This book will be an examination of the aspiration to rational self-sufficiency in Greek ethical thought: the aspiration to make the goodness of a good human life safe from luck through the

---

[3] See, for example, Francisco Gonzalez (ed.), *The Third Way: New Directions in Platonic Studies* (Lanham: Rowman & Littlefield, 1995).

[4] In recent scholarship, this theme has been especially developed by Pierre Hadot's very influential interpretation: Hadot, *Philosophy as a Way of Life* (Oxford & Cambridge: Blackwell Publishers, 1995), and Hadot, *What is Ancient Philosophy?* (Cambridge & London: Belknap Harvard, 2002).

controlling power of reason".[5] Nussbaum's specific analytical focus is on the vulnerable dimension of human goods, such as friendship, love, political conditions and property. She also raises questions regarding the relation between the rational and irrational parts of the soul.[6]

The relevance of these questions for current debate is obvious, especially during the 1980's when the book was written. Nussbaum thematizes the relation between reason and emotions, one of the central dualisms of modernity. Discussions concerning modern intellectualism have been ongoing since the late 18th century, but became prominent once more during the last decades of the 20th century, especially in connection with the dominance of Anglo-American analytical philosophy. *The Fragility of Goodness* deals with similar problems among the ancient Greeks. In this way, Nussbaum's approach turns out to be a critical inquiry into the western philosophical tradition. It also uncovers differences between ancient and modern philosophy, and has the ambition to detect alternative ways of dealing with fundamental questions concerning vulnerability.

∗∗∗

The general picture that Nussbaum paints of the ancient Greeks' struggle with the relationship between reason and emotions has a certain Hegelian tincture. She describes three phases or stages in its development. In classical tragedy, vulnerability and the impotence of reason are emphasized. In the next phase, Plato's philosophy is characterized by the opposite ideal: the self-sufficiency of reason. Finally, a sort of synthesis and balance between the two sides is formulated in Aristotle's ethics.[7]

This picture is highly generalized and it must be emphasized that there are a number of important nuances in Nussbaum's

---

[5] Nussbaum, *The Fragility of Goodness*, p. 3.
[6] Nussbaum, *The Fragility of Goodness*), p. 6.
[7] Nussbaum, *The Fragility of Goodness*, pp. 8 and 21.

narrative. Nonetheless, the overall interpretive pattern is present throughout the book. The framework lends her study a more dynamic historical dimension, and it presents philosophy as an activity engaged with real life problems. Moreover, it leads Nussbaum to a new appraisal of Greek philosophy and into polemics with other contemporary interpretations.[8]

For Nussbaum, Plato's philosophy is a form of intellectualism. He claims that human beings are capable of raising themselves above the irrational impulses of the soul through the use of reason, and that this rational control renders the soul self-sufficient and invulnerable. Nussbaum compares what she calls Plato's "intellectualist ethics" and to the pathos of analytical philosophy,[9] and uses this general interpretation of Plato's philosophy emblematically in many of her later works.[10]

In *The Fragility of Goodness*, however, the picture of Plato's philosophy is more nuanced and complex. Plato's dialogues are not analyzed simply as doctrines, but also as a reaction to established ideas about the human condition, particularly the tragic worldview. Hence Nussbaum reads Plato as an attempt to overcome the ethical problems of his time. She also pursues Plato's continued struggle with these issues, and here we find an innovative combination of traditional and more novel approaches.

The readings of Plato are traditional in a number of respects. First, Nussbaum reads Plato as having systematic philosophical ideas about Being, the cosmos and human nature. Second, she adheres to the view that these ideas are represented by the figure of Socrates in the written texts. Third, it is assumed that the differences between Socrates' statements in different dialogues mirror Plato's philosophical development.

Yet Nussbaum combine these traditional readings with a novel analysis of the literary form. She argues that the cultural

[8] Nussbaum, *The Fragility of Goodness*, pp. 18-19.
[9] Nussbaum, *The Fragility of Goodness*, pp. 15-16.
[10] For example in Nussbaum, *Love's Knowledge* (1990) and *Upheavals of Thought* (2001).

situation led Plato to choose the dialogue form as a new educational medium, a genre that combines philosophy and literature. The public debate was dominated by people who despised and rejected philosophy, and the dialogue form was created to criticize and reveal the shortcomings of both classical poets and sophists. For Plato, philosophy was an ongoing search for wisdom, and his texts focus more on ways to proceed than on the goal itself. In this project, the dialogue form can engage more than a presentation of general doctrines and pull the reader into the discussions and a quest for wisdom. According to Nussbaum, however, "Plato's anti-tragic theater" is a purely intellectual pursuit—emotional experiences play no significant role for insight.[11]

From this analysis of the literary form, Nussbaum draws the conclusion that any interpretation of the dialogues must adopt a historical and contextualizing approach. She aims to recover the philosophical thrust by investigating how the characters of the dialogues position themselves in their context. The ambition is to come closer to how 4th Century Athenians could have read the texts. To this end, Nussbaum provides lively portrayals of both the political and cultural conditions and the drama of the dialogues. It is on these points that, among other Plato exegetes, Nussbaum's interpretations have been received positively.

***

The main theme in Nussbaum's readings concerns Plato's ongoing struggle with the ethical problems of his time. She is especially occupied with his view of human vulnerability and the relation between reason and irrational desires. The interpretation that Nussbaum advances shows a philosophy in the making, and the dynamic evolution of Plato's theories and ideals.

Developmental interpretations of Plato's philosophy usually operate with three more or less distinct periods: early, middle and late. Within this general pattern, scholars may have different

---

[11] Nussbaum, *The Fragility of Goodness*, pp. 87-88 and 122-135.

versions and subdivisions. In adherence to these developmental perspectives, Nussbaum offers a new interpretation of Plato's philosophical evolution. She reads Socrates' arguments as expressions of Plato's position and traces his changing ethical views through four dialogues, stretching from the late early period to the early late period.

In the early *Protagoras*, Nussbaum finds an optimistic attempt to overcome human vulnerability. Socrates claims that the irrational desires of the soul can, at least in part, be educated by the intellect.[12] In the *Republic*, from the middle period, there is a modified and more pessimistic position. Socrates describes the most basic irrational desires as immutable and resistant to teaching. Because of this it is not enough to educate the irrational desires, they must be controlled and suppressed by reason, and even be put under political control.[13] This change in philosophical position, according to Nussbaum, is prefigured in the ambivalence of the drama of the *Protagoras*. Here Socrates is not the clear winner of the debate, with the antagonist Protagoras making a number of salient points. The ambivalence of this dialogue is read as an expression of an ambivalence that marks Plato's own philosophical views.[14] Nussbaum admits that her analysis is somewhat speculative, but argues that it is supported by a similar pattern in later dialogues.

In Plato's *Symposium*, the focus is on a single desire: *eros* or love. On Nussbaum's account, Socrates voices the same general position as he holds in the *Republic* concerning reason and irrational desires. In the *Symposium*, *eros* is transformed into a desire purified from irrational emotions, that is, into a purely intellectual love. In the famous ascent on the ladder of love, the disciple is persuaded by the teacher to abandon all individuality for a higher form of life. Socrates praises a love that amounts to

[12] Nussbaum, *The Fragility of Goodness*, pp. 89-121.
[13] Nussbaum, *The Fragility of Goodness*, pp. 135-164.
[14] Nussbaum, *The Fragility of Goodness*, pp. 121, 89-120, 135-164.

intellectual intercourse, one that is self-sufficient and free from any vulnerability.

This interpretation is well in line with our modern conception of Platonic love. Nussbaum's specific focus on the anti-individual and egotistic aspects of Socrates speech is also topical, contributing to the lively debate in Anglo-American scholarship during the latter half of the 20th century.[15] But her account also involves a number of more original elements. She offers unusually complex readings of the dramatic setting, placing the *Symposium* in both political and cultural contexts, especially Athens during the Peloponnesian War. There are observations and suggestions here that have since then become standard points of reference in scholarly discussions.[16]

As in the *Protagoras*, Socrates' victory in the *Symposium* is dubious. The protagonists Aristophanes and Alcibiades give strong arguments for their cases; Nussbaum suggests that their speeches portray an *eros* that takes individuality and vulnerability into account. Thus they constitute intra-dialogical challenges to Socrates' conception of love. Nussbaum sketches a systematic contrast between Socrates' and Alcibiades' speeches. Against the former's intellectual love for an abstract quality stands the latter's love for a concrete individual. Against a self-sufficiency of intellectual love stands a vulnerable passion. Against a deductive *episteme* stands an understanding through experience (*pathe gnonai*). According to Nussbaum, the speeches portray two ideals, but also two different kinds of knowledge that are irreducible to one another. In her view, the drama of the *Symposium* is an enactment of two types of philosophy competing for our souls. It is also an enactment of the philosophical

---

[15] Lorelle D. Lamascus, *The Poverty of Eros in Plato's Symposium* (London: Bloomsbury Academic, 2017), pp. 12-20.
[16] This is especially true for her analysis of the role of Alcibiades and politics in the dialogue, from the puzzling *prologos* to the ambivalent *epilogos*.

dimension of the political and cultural turmoil that Athens went through during the Peloponnesian War.[17]

Nussbaum interprets the two positions and ethical choices in the *Symposium* as a sign of ambivalence and an indication that Plato's philosophical stance is about to shift—again. This reading is confirmed in her analysis of the *Phaedrus*, Plato's later erotic dialogue. Here we find the two positions played out in quite a different way. There are, to be sure, three speeches on love in the *Phaedrus*, but the first two are essentially demonstrations of the same position. They criticize love as a socially and morally destructive madness, whereas Socrates' last speech praises love as a divine madness, one of the highest blessings available to humans. The two earlier speeches are severely criticized in Socrates last speech, which he characterizes as a disavowal. In Nussbaum's analysis, the first two speeches are versions of Plato's own earlier views on reason and desires as they are explained in the *Republic* and the *Symposium*. By extension, this last speech can be interpreted as Plato's self-criticism of his earlier philosophy.

According to Nussbaum, Socrates' second speech in the *Phaedrus*, in contrast to the *Symposium*, does not abstract from individuality. The lover reaches the form of beauty through the beloved individual, not by negating him. The relation between two lovers is at the very core of the love-experience. Furthermore, Socrates here does not portray all complex souls as corrupt or deficient. Quite the contrary, desires are not all blind animal forces, and especially not *eros*. The latter can function as a good motivational power, and even play a fundamental role in the philosophical life. The intellect is no longer seen as sufficient for achieving the highest insights.[18]

After having analyzed these changes in Plato's philosophy, Nussbaum raises the question of how they should be explained. She argues that there must have been some new powerful experi-

---

[17] Nussbaum, *The Fragility of Goodness*, pp. 197-198.
[18] Nussbaum, *The Fragility of Goodness*, pp. 221-225.

ences that led to this reevaluation of a fundamental philosophical position. Here she cites a love poem—attributed to Plato by the ancients—written as an epitaph to Dion of Syracuse, his long-time friend who was murdered. She argues that the *Phaedrus* alludes to Dion's and Plato's relationship. More importantly, the poem expresses grief and lack of self-sufficiency. Nussbaum admits, again, that all of this is rather speculative, but she explores it as a possibility and formulates a far-reaching psychological interpretation.[19]

> What happened to Plato, we are invited by his hints to conjecture, was that he discovered that merely human life was more complicated, but also richer or better, than he had imagined. Obviously he had been aware before this of the power of passion; what he had not seen so clearly was its power for goodness. He tells us that he was struck in all parts of his soul by the splendor of another whole person; being struck, he formed, and in this dialogue depicted, a close and exclusive relationship in which wonder, respect, passion, and careful concern all fostered, in both, the growth of philosophical insight. In this love between an older established person and a younger aspiring person, he found access to element of his own personality as a thinker and writer that he would before have derided as merely womanly, perhaps because they had too much to do with passivity.[20]

***

There are a number of things that can be questioned or discussed in Nussbaum's analysis. Here, I will focus on three major points: the concept of reason in Plato; the psychological perspectives she offers; and the interpretation of his intellectual development.

Nussbaum's analysis of the dichotomy between reason and desires/emotions is both interesting and problematic. As an analysis of its role in modern culture, especially classical positivism and analytical philosophy, it raises a number of good points con-

---

[19] Nussbaum, *The Fragility of Goodness*, pp. 228-232.
[20] Nussbaum, *The Fragility of Goodness*, pp. 230-131.

cerning "love's knowledge". However, as an analysis of Plato's dialogues, it is not without its problems. Despite Nussbaum's awareness of differences between ancient and modern concepts, there appears to be a certain degree of projection of the modern dichotomy onto the ancient texts. Her analysis of Plato's intellectualism is queerly reminiscent of modern intellectualism.

There are at least two problems here. First, Nussbaum does not do justice to the ancient concept of noetic reason. When Plato talks about knowledge of forms, he uses primarily visual metaphors: seeing, perceiving, receiving, the inner eye of the soul etc. Knowledge of the forms is therefore not primarily of a conceptual nature, but a kind of intellectual vision and clarity. Second, Nussbaum does not see the erotic side of the Platonic concept of reason, nor, conversely, the rational side of desires as they are portrayed also in the *Republic* and the *Symposium*. Her analysis of Platonic love as directed toward an abstract intellectual quality is therefore misguided. On Platonic premises, the perception of the forms is not a question of intellectual abstraction, but an inner vision of the natural forms of the world.[21]

These issues are not just problems of scholarship, but also of relevance. With an interpretation that partly projects modern conceptions and dichotomies onto ancient philosophy, we forfeit the possibility of a deeper philosophical and cultural contrast. A continued analysis of differences might have given us a clearer view of both the shortcomings and advantages of our modern way of thinking.[22]

---

[21] For a general overview of interpretations of the platonic forms and Plato's concept of reason, see William A. Welton (ed.), *Plato's Forms: Varieties of Interpretation* (Lanham: Rowman & Littlefield, 2002). For an example of a sophisticated account that discusses the relation to modern concepts, see Stanley Rosen, *The Question of Being* (New Haven & London: Yale University Press, 1993), pp. 15, 51-55, 68-71, 93-96.

[22] Michael Frede, "Introduction" in Michael Frede & Gisela Striker (eds.), *Rationality in Greek Thought* (Oxford: Clarendon, 1996), pp. 5-9. Charles Kahn, "Plato's Theory of Desire", *Review of Metaphysics* 41 (1987-1988), pp. 77-103. Dimitrios Iordanoglou & Mats Persson, "In the Midst of Demons: Eros and Temporality in Plato's *Symposium*", in Ingela Nilsson (ed.), *Plot-*

As we have seen, Nussbaum makes frequent use of dramatic readings of the Platonic dialogues. Her psychological interpretations of the characters and their motives, however, often tend to overshadow the philosophical dimensions. Other dramatic interpretations have put philosophical arguments of Socrates and others in the context of the literary drama to deepen the understanding of the philosophizing conducted therein. Socrates' claims and arguments are investigated in relation to the questions and debates at hand and, in this way, they are modified and limited. It has even been suggested that Plato intentionally uses fallacies in his texts, even in the speeches of the character of Socrates.[23] Nussbaum's readings rarely take account of such elements. To be sure, she does analyze arguments, but the interpretations tend to be psychological. She argues, for example, that Alcibiades' speech modifies Socrates' teaching in the *Symposium*. But this is interpreted as expressing Plato's psychological ambivalence and the prefiguring of a future philosophical shift.

It is not always clear what Nussbaum's psychological analysis of the characters of the dialogue adds to the philosophical argument. Alcibiades' speech is interpreted as an expression of confusion, disappointment, jealousy and vulnerability. Thus Alcibiades is portrayed as subject to irrational passions and fortune, something that was played out in Alcibiades' political and military career, with catastrophic consequences for himself and for Athenian democracy. It is not clear just what Nussbaum's claim is here. She speaks of Plato's strategies, but also hints that the character of Alcibiades in the dialogue is an expression of Plato's

---

ting with Eros: *Essays on the Poetics of Love and the Erotics of Reading* (Copenhagen: Museeum Tusculanum Press, 2009), pp. 17-43.

[23] For clarifying examples concerning Plato's *Symposium*, see Michael C. Stokes, *Plato's Socratic Conversations* (Baltimore: Johns Hopkins University Press, 1986), pp. 114-182. A classical study of Plato's use of fallacy as a part of Socratic dialectic, see Rosamond Kent Sprague, *Plato's Use of Fallacy: A Study of the Euthydemus and Some other Dialogues* (London 1962), especially, pp. xiff, 80-88.

own experiences. As a rule, psychological explanation takes precedence in Nussbaum's readings.[24]

As we have seen, the psychological perspective is also present in the analysis of Plato's philosophical development. While chronological interpretations of Plato's philosophy are by no means something specific to Nussbaum, the psychological approach she adopts certainly is. She explains Plato's philosophical changes by his new experiences, where the latter are extracted through the readings that Nussbaum offers of the dialogues. New emotional experiences of *eros* have made Plato question his earlier belief in the power and self-sufficiency of reason and thus led him to develop new philosophical theories.

There are a number of issues at hand here. Until recently, the developmental interpretation has often functioned as the dominant paradigm for much of Plato scholarship. In the last few decades, however, this paradigm has increasingly been criticized. To begin with, the very idea of reading Plato's dialogues as expressions of a philosophical evolution is itself a modern one. It dates back to the middle of the 19th century, the epoch of evolutionary thinking; before that, no one even considered it. This is not in itself a decisive argument, but it is a legitimate concern. At the very least, the critique opens up room for discussion: whether or not Plato changed his mind about fundamentals over time is and must remain an open question. Another worry about the developmental view is that there are indications that Plato rewrote some of his dialogues. A further matter is the assumption that the dialogues were written as presentations of doctrines; it has been argued that Plato intended them rather as philosophical exercises for different audiences and readers at different levels of philosophical training.[25]

---

[24] Nussbaum, *The Fragility of Goodness*, pp. 189-198.

[25] For a discussion of many types of problems and alternatives, see Holger Thesleff, *Studies in Platonic Chronology* (Helsinki: Societas Scientiarum Fennica, 1982). For an overall critique of chronological-developmental interpretations, see Jacob Howland, "Re-Reading Plato: The Problem of Platonic

A related problem concerns Nussbaum's doctrinal readings. Her interpretations presuppose that the Platonic dialogues were written as general theories or principles. If the dialogues are instead read as discussions dealing with different questions, as is indicated in the dramatic framing, then this will account for certain differences and inconsistencies between different texts. In the *Symposium*, for instance, there is a speech contest, and, furthermore, Socrates states that it is in the nature of an *encomium* to pick out beautiful truths. In the *Phaedrus*, on the other hand, the context is a problem concerning the relation between a lover and a beloved from a moral point of view. It is not at all clear that the differences in content between the two dialogues are due to a change of heart on Plato's part. Nor is it obvious that the role of individuality is different in the two dialogues. The focus on this question seems to be Nussbaum's concern, rather than Plato's.

***

In the end, the problems run deep. Nussbaum's analysis seems to presuppose both modern philosophical problems and modern psychology. In her analysis, Plato is struggling with the relationship between reason and emotions in the same way as modern intellectuals do. Ultimately, the entire interpretation of Plato's development is formed by modern moral and psychological presuppositions.

Let us take the example of love. For Nussbaum, love should be directed toward individuals and not be egoistic; the beloved should be valued for his or her own sake. This is a moral conviction, but there also seems to be a psychological claim about what love is by nature. This comes to light in her analysis of the changes in Plato's views from the *Republic* and the *Symposium*, where *eros* is directed towards an abstract intellectual quality, to

Chronology", *Phoenix*, vol. 45 (1991), and Francisco Gonzalez, "Eros and Dialectic in Plato's Phaedrus: Questioning the Value of Chronology", in Debra Nails & Harold Tarrant (eds.), *Second Sailing: Alternative Perspectives on Plato* (Helsinki: Societas Scientiarum Fennica, 2015).

the *Phaedrus*, where there is a reevaluation of love directed towards an individual. Plato, Nussbaum claims, had experiences that made him call into question his earlier philosophical views. Her explanatory principle here is that individuality is at the heart of love, and the denial of this point is psychologically untenable.

These moral and psychological presuppositions also inform Nussbaum's analysis of Plato struggle with the relation between intellect and emotions. According to Nussbaum, he moves from believing in the possibility of educating the irrational passions to recommending their suppression, and, finally, to a new understanding of their positive potential. Moreover, it was life experiences that taught him and led him to make philosophical changes. Indeed, Nussbaum offers a similar interpretation of classical Greek culture as a whole. In tragedy, reason is powerless; in Plato, it is omnipotent. Finally, in Aristotle, we find a balance between reason and emotions. In each case, an unbalanced relation drives the intellectual search for an ethical and cultural solution.

These interpretations rest upon a couple of modern presuppositions. Firstly, that love is by nature non-egoistic and directed toward unique individuals. Secondly, that there is a natural balance between reason and emotion. Failure to adhere to these principles causes problems in life. In Nussbaum's narrative, these presuppositions seem to be moral and ontological at the same time. As we have seen, however, the application (or rather, projection) of these categories onto Plato and ancient Greek culture is neither historically, philologically or conceptually self-evident. Rather, such an approach reveals a modern humanist ideal, one that is problematic as a portrayal of human nature.

Nussbaum, Aristotle, and the Problem of Anthropocentrism

Charlotta Weigelt

"Nothing feebler does earth nurture than man, of all things that on earth breathe and move."[1] This is Odysseus speaking to Amphinomus, a man whom he is about to kill, since Amphinomus belongs to the party of suitors that has been besieging his home during his absence. In view of Odysseus' immediate plans, it is a particularly appropriate time for him to remind Amphinomous of the fragility of human life: that our fortune can change at any moment. I do not know whether Nussbaum ever cites this passage from the *Odyssey* (given her immense productivity, it is practically impossible to tell), but I think it aptly captures one of the more central convictions behind her ethical project, not to say of her philosophical outlook as a whole. In *The Fragility of Goodness* from 1986,[2] her first major work after her doctoral dissertation on Aristotle's *De Motu Animalium*,[3] Nussbaum argues at great length that the good life essentially involves an ability to affirm one's own finitude and vulnerability,

---

[1] Homer, *Odyssey*, trans. A. T. Murray, rev. George E. Dimock (Cambridge, MA.: Harvard University Press, 2004, 2. ed.), 18.130-131.

[2] Martha Nussbaum, *The Fragility of Goodness: Luck and Ethics in Greek Tragedy and Philosophy* (Cambridge: Cambridge University Press, 1986).

[3] Nussbaum, *Aristotle's* De Motu Animalium: *Text with Translation, Commentary, and Interpretive Essays* (Princeton: Princeton University Press, 1978).

as opposed to wanting to master the human condition, in the sense of trying to find protection from the external and uncontrollable forces that by necessity shape the life of every human being. Striving for autonomy in that sense amounts to nothing less than denying exactly what makes us human. And it is by and large the conviction that Aristotle is an exemplary thinker in this respect, that is to say, that his ethics is founded on an insight into the fragility of human luck and happiness, that makes Nussbaum turn to Aristotle as her most important philosophical compatriot in several of her works.

Nussbaum's ethical stance also has an important epistemological dimension. A recurrent assumption in her work is that we have no option but to search for the criteria for the good life within the human realm itself, among our extant norms and beliefs. "Our questions about the good life must, like any question whatever, be asked and answered within the appearances."[4] Indeed, we are mistaken if we believe that ethics even would gain anything by the existence of an objective measure that transcends the human condition. In Nussbaum's view, one of the merits of Aristotle's ethics is precisely that it refrains from positing any absolute values that would govern our lives from outside, so to speak. For this reason, it may rightfully be called an anthropocentric ethics. Another reason for labeling Aristotle's ethics as anthropocentric is that his notion of good is species-relative, as Nussbaum calls it: it deals with precisely the human good, and nothing else, guided by the conviction that the good, *to agathon*, is not a unified concept to begin with.[5]

As can be seen already in her work on *De Motu Animalium*, however, Nussbaum also wants to make the stronger claim that Aristotle's entire work is anthropocentric in the sense that even his more scientifically oriented philosophy, not just his ethics, is guided by the conviction that the truth about the world must be

---

[4] Nussbaum, *The Fragility of Goodness*, p. 291.
[5] Nussbaum, *The Fragility of Goodness*, pp. 291-292.

sought within the framework of man's various interpretations of that world.[6] So even when we do not deal with a specifically human phenomenon, we remain within the confines of human intelligibility. In one of the essays contained in her book on *De Motu Animalium* that is dedicated to Aristotle's methodology, Nussbaum spells out the implications of his position as follows:

> There is no sharp line between the "scientific" and the "meta-physical," between what can be demonstrated and that of which we simply say "let it underlie"; it is neither helpful nor wise to separate the "scientific" questions from those that rest on our intuitions and interpretations. The scientific depends on what appears, and what looks most solid is so not because it is free from interpretation, but because it is based on the most universal and fundamental interpretations.[7]

Nussbaum is far from the only contemporary thinker who has wanted to rehabilitate Aristotle's methodology in order to acquire an ally in an attempt to come to grips with some of the major philosophical challenges of today. Nor is she alone in thinking that the *Nicomachean Ethics* is a good place to start in this pursuit, due to the belief that Aristotle here shows us the way out of certain philosophical impasses, offering us an alternative to, or a position in between, scientism and irrationalism, and also in between communitarianism and liberalism, to just mention two of the most debated issues in contemporary philosophy in which Aristotle has made his mark. In the Anglo-Saxon or analytic philosophical tradition, to which Nussbaum herself belongs, people like Hilary Putnam, Alasdair MacIntyre and John McDowell have turned to Aristotle for similar reasons.[8] In the so-called Continental tradi-

---

[6] See also Nussbaum, *The Fragility of Goodness*, pp. 242-243.

[7] Nussbaum, "Essay 2: the *De Motu Animalium* and Aristotle's Scientific Method", *Aristotle's* De Motu Animalium, p. 137.

[8] See Alasdair MacIntyre, *After Virtue: A Study in Moral Theory* (London: Duckworth, 1981) and John McDowell, *Mind and World* (Cambridge, MA: Harvard University Press, 1996). Among Hilary Putnam's many works, especially relevant in this connection is the article he co-authored with

tion, the most well-known readers of Aristotle in this respect are Martin Heidegger, Hannah Arendt and Hans-Georg Gadamer.[9]

One of the major lessons of the *Nicomachean Ethics* is that, on the one hand, we will distort the essential characteristics of the life of action if we try to judge it by the yardstick given to us by science, believing that this life obeys rules and principles which could be made completely transparent, but that, on the other hand, this predicament does not entail that human morality is simply a matter of discretion, without any rational basis at all. Aristotle's concept of *phronēsis*, the power of judgment in practical matters, has attracted particular attention among his modern readers because it is thought to make clear how it is indeed possible to attain knowledge of particulars, albeit not scientific knowledge, which concerns the universal. Rather, the kind of knowledge that is the province of *phronēsis* is an application of universal moral principles onto the particular situation of action, in such a way that the former, the universal dimension of morality, is shown to acquire sense and concretion only as it is realized in the particular situation.[10] What Aristotle has achieved, in other words, is a solution to Plato's problem of *methexis*: he

Nussbaum, which is a defense of what the authors label as Aristotle's functionalism with respect to the mind-body problem; see "Changing Aristotle's Mind", *Essays on Aristotle's* De Anima, eds. M. C. Nussbaum & A. Oksenberg Rorty (Oxford: Oxford University Press, 1995), pp. 27-56. An informative survey of contemporary Aristotelian thinkers, with a focus on analytic philosophy, is John R. Wallach, "Contemporary Aristotelianism", *Political Theory* 20:4 (1992), pp. 613-641. See also Thomas Gutschker, *Aristotelische Diskurse: Aristoteles in der politischen Philosophie des 20. Jahrhunderts* (Stuttgart: Metzler, 2002), which deals with the reception of Aristotle in both the analytic and the Continental tradition.

[9] During the 1920s, Heidegger devoted several courses to Aristotle, but see in particular *Plato's* Sophist, trans. R. Rojcewicz & A. Schuwer (Bloomington: Indiana University Press, 1997) for his interpretation of Aristotle's ethics. See also Hannah Arendt, *The Human Condition* (Chicago: The University of Chicago Press, 1998) and Hans-Georg Gadamer, *Truth and Method*, trans. J. Weinsheimer & D. G. Marshall (London & New York: Continuum, 2004).

[10] Aristotle, *Nicomachean Ethics* VI.5 and 1141b14-22.

has shown that the application of "ideas" onto the realm of change is not to be construed in terms of distortion and simulacrum but as adaptation in a positive sense. The mediation between universal and particular simply is a constitutive aspect of man's interpretation of his world, not just of the ethical realm.[11]

One way of describing the reason behind the turn to Aristotle in 20th century philosophy, which moreover continues to this day, is that he seems to hold out a promise for a cure to that disease which Nietzsche predicted would fall upon man with the death of God, that is to say, with the loss of absolute values and, more broadly speaking, of a transcendent measure for human morality, that is, the contagion of nihilism. Against this dark diagnosis, Aristotle shows that there is still something to be said on the question concerning right and wrong, namely that we are not only obliged to, but actually can justify our courses of action in a rational way.

To claim, in the manner of Nussbaum and others, that Aristotle, the father of empirical science, in fact does not endorse metaphysical realism and, thus, does not believe that reality simply is what it is "in itself", independent of human theories and interpretations, is still controversial.[12] Considering that Aristotle does not play a particularly insignificant role in the history of philosophy and science, to say the least, this kind of reinterpretation of his work is hardly merely a concern for historians. Rather, it is a struggle about our tradition that concerns the nature and scope of its legacy. As such, it is also a struggle about our own age. What drives Nussbaum and other "Neo-Aristotelians" is at least in part the prospect of being able to give historical weight to

---

[11] Gadamer is particularly clear about this; see *Truth and Method*, pp. 310-321.

[12] The question concerning the tenability of this interpretation of Aristotle is one I will not pursue here. For an extensive criticism of Nussbaum on this point, see Jack D. Davidson, "Appearances, Antirealism, and Aristotle", *Philosophical Studies: An International Journal for Philosophy in the Analytic Tradition* 63:2 (1991), pp. 147-166. See also Gutschker, *Aristotelische Diskurse*, p. 437.

their own thinking, also in order to show that they themselves belong to the right camp. And at least in the case of Nussbaum, it is perfectly clear who is the major representative of the rival camp, namely Plato. His philosophy is the origin of the scientism that haunts the present age. More precisely, Plato introduced the hope that it would be possible to find a *technē*, a craft or a technique, with the aid of which the vulnerability of human life could be possible to master. In *The Fragility of Goodness*, Nussbaum argues that Plato's thought is continuous with that of his tragic predecessors in so far as he too saw the human predicament for what it was, namely, being exposed to *tuchē*: to luck, contingency and fate.[13] But there the continuity ends. In his ethical reflections, Plato develops the distinction between *tuchē* and *technē* into an ideal of a self-sufficient human life, where *technē* gets the upper hand on *tuchē*.[14]

In Plato, as Nussbaum reads him, the capability to act is not so much a capability to respond to the particular challenges and needs of life but rather the capacity to avoid the confrontation with them to begin with, thanks to the controlling powers of *technē*. We may note in passing that Nussbaum's emphasis on *technē* as a key concept in Plato's ethics is not particularly controversial in itself. Especially in the supposedly early, so-called Socratic dialogues, Socrates constantly employs analogies with the crafts, such as carpentry, horse breeding and medicine, when discussing the nature of virtue, *aretē*. What makes Nussbaum's interpretation stand out in this context is her dismissive attitude toward the Platonic project of taking rational control over our moral lives.[15] As already indicated, in her view, Plato's ethics turns away from what is distinctively human, and this move has

---

[13] The Greek word *tuchē* can take on all these meanings. Nussbaum translates it for the most part as "luck".

[14] Nussbaum, *The Fragility of Goodness*, pp. 89, 97.

[15] For a diametrically opposed evaluation of the role of *technē* in the early dialogues, see Daniel W. Graham, "Socrates, the Craft Analogy, and Science", *Apeiron* 24:1 (1991), pp. 1-24.

bearings for his understanding of knowledge in general. Both practical and theoretical knowledge aim at mastery by subduing the human perspective: "The ability to go outside of shared human conceptions and beliefs is here [...] made a necessary condition of access to the real truth about our lives. The perfect god's-eye standpoint is the only reliable one from which to make adequate and reliably true judgments."[16]

Nussbaum thus retrieves the old conflict between Plato and Aristotle in order to be able to deal with the present situation, where the major challenge, as she sees it, consists in finding a middle way between objectivism and subjectivism, that is to say, to demonstrate the possibility of a rational (non-relativistic) discourse on ethical matters that does not seek justification in anything that is external to or beyond the confines of human evaluation.[17] Her reply to that challenge is precisely anthropocentrism, not only in the sense of affirming the point of view from within, but also as an attempt to base ethics on an idea of what is characteristic of human nature, as we shall soon see. Nussbaum's position has been criticized on the grounds that it is itself a form of subjectivism or relativism.[18] As far as I can see, however, the critique stems at least in part from an inability, which charac-

---

[16] Nussbaum, *The Fragility of Goodness*, p. 242. Nussbaum's verdict on Plato comes pretty close to that pronounced by Arendt, who similarly regards the theory of ideas as an attempt to deprive man of the power to judge in ethical and political matters, by introducing a set of absolute values that makes such judgment not only superfluous but also impossible. To Arendt, however, it is important to distinguish this Platonic move from the Socratic ethics of the early dialogues. See "Socrates", *The Promise of Politics*, ed. Jerome Kohn (New York: Schocken Books, 2005), pp. 5-39.

[17] Nussbaum gives different formulations of this contrast. In *Aristotle's De Motu Animalium*, she explains that Aristotle has circumscribed "a middle ground between sophistic relativism and scientific deductivism", p. 219. In another context, she introduces her own essentialism as an alternative to both metaphysical realism and subjectivism; "Human Functioning and Social Justice: In Defense of Aristotelian Essentialism", *Political Theory* 20:2 (1992), p. 209.

[18] Gutschker, *Aristotelische Diskurse*, pp. 439-440; Davidson, "Appearances, Antirealism, and Aristotle".

terizes much analytic philosophy, to realize how an acknowledgement of the human subject's participation in the givenness of the world could lead to anything but to an abandonment of the notion of objectivity as such, and therewith also of the very idea of a single, common world.[19]

To many people, "anthropocentrism" has a decidedly negative connotation: it is associated with a notion of being trapped inside the human sphere, which is problematic both in an ethical sense (one looks upon man as the peak of creation) and epistemologically (one assumes that the human perspective is the only correct one). In short, one makes man into the measure of all things, as the great sophist Protagoras, one of Plato's contemporaries, is believed to have held. Nussbaum herself would in all likelihood not be prepared to admit that she is vulnerable to this kind of objections, but I shall suggest at the end of this article that she has at least not refuted them in an altogether satisfactory way.

In any case, what Nussbaum is aiming at for her own part is a position that is also labeled "internalism", as opposed to "externalism". One of Nussbaum's philosophical compatriots, Hilary Putnam, introduced the expression "internal realism" so as to emphasize that the implication of the internalist position is not some version or other of metaphysical idealism (according to which the world is the product of subjectivity). Rather, it is based on the conviction that what is real has its sense of reality only in relation to subjective experience, or in other words: reality is not something that lies beyond possible experience, and in that sense it is not anything external in relation to us that would affect us

---

[19] Gottlob Frege, the father of analytic philosophy, was no doubt decisive in this respect, when he declared that sense (*Sinn*), even though it is the mode of givenness (*Art des Gegebenseins*) of the object, is not in any way constituted by the subject's conception of the object, which Frege identifies with the internal and subjective image of the world studied by psychology (as opposed to philosophy and logic). See "Sense and Reference", *The Philosophical Review* 57:3 (1948), pp. 209-230.

behind our backs, so to speak.[20] Occasionally, Nussbaum describes her view of human nature as an "internal essentialism",[21]
and I shall return to it shortly.

At the time Nussbaum wrote *The Fragility of Goodness*, she
did not use this label to characterize Aristotle's position, but it is
clear, as was also indicated above, that she reads him as an internal realist.[22] Here she sums up Aristotle's position as follows:

> Appearances and truth are not opposed, as Plato believed they
> were. We can have truth only *inside* the circle of the appearan-
> ces, because only there can we communicate, even refer at all.
> This, then – if we may characterize it for ourselves using lan-
> guage not known to Aristotle himself – is a kind of realism,
> neither idealism of any sort nor skepticism. [...] It is a realism,
> however, that articulates very carefully the limits within which
> any realism must live.[23]

It is fairly obvious that Aristotle is a kind of internalist at least in
his ethics. In the *Nicomachean Ethics* he repeatedly states that
the horizon of his inquiry into morality is provided by the
human perception of morality, rather than by some absolute
standard, such as Plato's idea of the good.[24] The measure (*met-
ron*) and the precept (*kanōn*), more precisely, are the good man,

---

[20] See Putnam, "Two philosophical perspectives", *Reason, Truth, and History*
(Cambridge: Cambridge University Press, 1981), pp. 49-74. Eventually, however, Putnam abandoned his own version of internal realism, coming to the
conclusion that, after all, it entails precisely idealism. See *The Threefold
Cord: Mind, Body, and World* (New York: Columbia University Press, 1999),
pp. 13, 17-18.

[21] Nussbaum, "Human Functioning and Social Justice", p. 208; "Aristotle,
Politics, and Human Capabilities: A Response to Antony, Arneson, Charles-
worth, and Mulgan", *Ethics* 111:1 (2000), p. 119.

[22] In an article written only a few years later, Nussbaum refers in a note to
chapter 8 of *The Fragility of Goodness*, "Saving Aristotle's appearances", with
the comment "on Aristotle's 'internal realism', see Nussbaum, *Fragility*,
chap. 8". See "Non-Relative Virtues: An Aristotelian Approach", *Midwest
Studies in Philosophy* XIII (1988), p. 52, n. 30.

[23] Nussbaum, *The Fragility of Goodness*, p. 257.

[24] Aristotle, *Nicomachean Ethics* I.6.

not the good as such.[25] There is one passage in the *Nicomachean Ethics* related to this issue that Nussbaum cites on several occasions, apparently a favorite of hers. Here Aristotle is discussing our emotional life, and especially lack of self-restraint, *akrasia*, and adds a reflection concerning his own method:

> We must, as in all other cases, set the phenomena before us and, after first discussing the difficulties, go on to prove, if possible, the truth of all the reputable opinions (*ta endoxa*) about these affections or, failing this, of the greater number and the most authoritative; for if we both resolve the difficulties and leave the reputable opinions undisturbed, we shall have proved the case sufficiently. (1145b2-7)[26]

Here Aristotle thus establishes commonly accepted opinions, *endoxa*, as a measure within the space of norms. In connection with ethical questions, this might seem like a completely reasonable, not to say obvious line of approach: where else should we turn to learn about good and evil in human conduct, if not to the human context? On the other hand, though, if all we have by way of measure is different opinions about the good life, how can we rationally argue that one opinion is better in the sense of more justified than another? As Nussbaum knows very well, Aristotle's "good" man did not hesitate to keep slaves, and he believed that the Greeks were superior to all other people and that the proper place for women was the household.[27] In Nussbaum's view, this

---

[25] Aristotle, *Nicomachean Ethics* 1113a33, 1166a12, 1176a18.

[26] Trans. W. D. Ross (rev. J. O. Urmson), *The Complete Works of Aristotle*, vol. II, ed. Jonathan Barnes (Princeton: Princeton University Press, 1995). The passage is cited by Nussbaum in *The Fragility of Goodness*, p. 240; "Aristotle on human nature and the foundations of ethics", *World, Mind, and Ethics: Essays on the Ethical Philosophy of Bernard Williams*, ed. J. E. J. Altham & Ross Harrison (Cambridge: Cambridge University Press, 1995), p. 102, and in *Aristotle's* De Motu Animalium, p. xvi, 105, 134.

[27] See Aristotle, *Politics* I.1, III.14 and VII.7. Nussbaum touches upon this topic in several of her articles on Aristotle, but see in particular "Aristotelian Social Democracy", *Liberalism and the Good*, eds. R. Bruce Douglass, Gerald Mara & Henry Richardson (New York: Routledge, 1990), pp. 203-253. See

is just Aristotle making "silly and unfounded judgments about barbarians and women", thus misapplying his own theory.[28] Here, then, "the Aristotelian must depart from Aristotle".[29] But even granted that there is nothing intrinsically unacceptable or at least problematic with Aristotle's ethics,[30] the question remains: if we think that his views on women, slaves and "barbarians" are nothing but unfounded prejudices, by what rights do we today consider ourselves less prejudiced than Aristotle?

Nussbaum gives two answers to this question. As already indicated, she does not think that the loss of a transcendent measure really is a loss at all:

> When we give up the hope of a transcendent metaphysical grounding for our evaluative judgments – about the human being as about anything else – we are not left with an abyss. We have everything that we always had all along: the exchange of reasons and arguments by human beings within history, in which, for reasons which are historical and human but not the worse for that, we hold some things to be good and others bad, some arguments to be sound and others not sound.[31]

Human discourse is the medium, so to speak, where we can let different opinions and norms confront and challenge each other. In this way, we get an opportunity to see our own position in the light of another, which can put us and our way of life into ques-

---

also "Aristotle on Human Nature and the Foundation of Ethics", and "Nature, Function and Capability: Aristotle on Political Distribution", *Wider Working Papers* (Helsinki 1987), pp. 1-50.

[28] Nussbaum, "Aristotle on human nature and the foundations of ethics", p. 122.

[29] Nussbaum, "Aristotelian Social Democracy", p. 239.

[30] For a critique of Nussbaum's project in this respect, see Manuel Knoll, *Aristokratische oder Demokratische Gerechtigkeit? Die politische Philosophie des Aristoteles und Martha Nussbaums egalitaristische Rezeption* (Munich: Fink, 2009), p. 211.

[31] Nussbaum, "Human Functioning and Social Justice", pp. 212-213.

tion.[32] This is, by the way, one reason that Nussbaum gives for her own interest in ancient philosophy.[33]

In *The Fragility of Goodness* Nussbaum raises herself the objection of circularity in connection with Aristotle's approach: "The standpoint of the person of practical wisdom [...] is definitive of value, and this value would not be value but for its relation to this human person." But if this is indeed the case, she continues, "how do we characterize this person and his procedures in a way that does not already make reference to the good content of his choices?"[34] As one might suspect, Nussbaum's answer is that there is no non-circular way of characterizing the competent ethical judge, for example by reference to supposedly value-neutral abilities, like imagination and empathy, as suggested by John Rawls.[35] Aristotle's intellectual abilities are not value-neutral, as Nussbaum rightly observes; on the contrary, they are virtues, as is clear from the beginning of *Nicomachean Ethics* VI. What Aristotle has at his disposal, however, is a wide range of human capacities that do not coincide with ethical competence but can be used to throw light on the ethical judge. These are, generally speaking, the crafts, favored in the ethical context not only by Plato but also by Aristotle, as is clear to every reader of the *Nicomachean Ethics*. In short, the point is that also in the crafts we are dealing with one or other conception of the good; there is, for example, a difference between a good and a bad doctor, and the question raised by both Plato and Aristotle is whether or not we can understand virtuous conduct in analogy with skill. When drawing upon these other competences, Aristotle is at least making the circle more complex and enlarging it, Nussbaum remarks.[36] In sum, then, the fact that we have to dig

---

[32] See Nussbaum, "Non-Relative Virtues", p. 47.

[33] Nussbaum, "Aristotle, Politics, and Human Capabilities", pp. 103-104.

[34] Nussbaum, *The Fragility of Goodness*, p. 311.

[35] John Rawls, "Outline for a Decision Procedure for Ethics", *Philosophical Review* 60 (1951), pp. 177-197. Nussbaum refers to Rawls' article in *The Fragility of Goodness*, p. 311.

[36] Nussbaum, *The Fragility of Goodness*, p. 312.

where we stand does not mean that the digging itself becomes meaningless.

But at the same time, Nussbaum claims that (and this is her second answer) if we want to avoid relativism in ethics, we need a common point of reference in the form of an idea of human nature. How, exactly, we are to conceive of human nature is a question that will occupy Nussbaum from the end of the 80's and onwards, but already in *The Fragility of Goodness*, the idea is present that the good life which we are seeking must be attainable by us as humans. Precisely this conviction drove Aristotle to distinguish between distinct forms of good, Nussbaum suggests. Since the goal of his ethics is practical, "there is no point to talking about the good life in an ethical inquiry insofar as this life is not practically attainable by creatures with our capabilities".[37] This idea is later developed into a more strongly articulated conviction that our nature sets limits for our morality.[38] Accordingly, ethics must be based on what Nussbaum labels "essentialism" and describes as the view that "human life has certain defining features", adding that the kind of essentialism that she wants to defend is "a historically sensitive account of the most basic human needs and human functions".[39] And it is Aristotle's view of human nature that she wants to rely upon, for reasons that will soon become clear. To want to deduce norms from nature, or ought from is, has been regarded with suspicion at least since Hume's days, and Nussbaum has also been criticized for this move.[40] On the surface, it might look like an attempt to provide morality with an objective foundation, not to say subject it to a complete naturalization. And it is pretty obvious that there

[37] Nussbaum, *The Fragility of Goodness*, pp. 292-293.
[38] Stated particularly clearly in Nussbaum, "Aristotle on Human Nature and the Foundations of Ethics", p. 91.
[39] Nussbaum, "Human Functioning and Social Justice", p. 205.
[40] See Louise M. Antony, "Natures and Norms", *Ethics* 111:1 (2000), pp. 8-36, who argues that Nussbaum fails to establish the alleged connection between humanity as a biological category and our views of what makes life worth living.

are several facts about our nature that we are not prepared to set up as norms. It might very well be the case that it is in our nature to be predators aiming primarily at survival, but that does not entail that it is right to eat other animals, pollute the environment, and so on. But, Nussbaum says, this is not her point. The nature she and Aristotle are talking about is not some brute fact that delimits us from the outside but is itself a normative concept, that is to say, an assessment of what is important in the life of a human being.[41] And that is something that all, or at least most of us can agree upon, irrespective of differences in, for example, gender, ethnicity and religious belief.[42]

The Aristotelian background to Nussbaum's argument is the teleological distinction between potentiality and actuality (*dunamis* and *energeia*), or in the terms used by Nussbaum, between capability and functioning. In the first book of the *Nicomachean Ethics*, Aristotle suggests that the question concerning the nature of happiness, *eudaimonia*, might become clearer if we could first ascertain the "work" or function (*ergon*) of man. Thus, he continues, "for all things that have a function and an activity [*praxis*], the good and the 'well' [*to eu*] is thought to reside in the function" (1097b26-27),[43] and therefore, the same must apply to man, granted that he indeed has a function. Having dismissed such features that are common to other organisms, such as life, nutrition, growth and perception, Aristotle concludes that the *ergon* of man is "an active life of the element that has a rational principle [*logos*]" (1098a3-4).[44] Already in the book on *De Motu Animalium*, Nussbaum devotes an appendix to this passage, noting, with approval, that the implication is that, before we begin to search for the good life, we must ask ourselves what a

[41] Nussbaum, "Human Functioning and Social Justice", p. 214; "Aristotle, Politics, and Human Capabilities", p. 118; "Aristotle on Human Nature and the Foundations of Ethics", p. 94.
[42] Nussbaum, "Aristotelian Social Democracy", p. 208.
[43] Trans. Ross (rev. Urmson).
[44] Trans. Ross (rev. Urmson).

human being is.[45] And she concludes her reflection on the *ergon* passage by stating that: "We want a life that uses all our capacities. Such a life both includes the exercise of reason and requires rational direction."[46]

The observation that Aristotle distinguishes man from other forms of life by referring to his function (rather than to his biological make-up), which in its turn is understood as a certain capacity (or perhaps rather as a set of capacities) that can be exercised in different ways, will later be instrumental to Nussbaum's co-called capabilities approach in both ethics and political philosophy. In this respect, it is also important that Aristotle's teleology allows us to demarcate capabilities from their various forms of actualization. In Aristotle's view, all capacities that involve some kind of rational element, that is to say, those capacities we do not simply possess but can relate to in different ways, which include not merely our capacity for thinking but also, to some extent, our faculty of sense perception, our emotional life and, not least, our ethical judgment, can be developed or realized in different directions for the sake of different purposes.[47] As a consequence, Aristotle cannot, strictly speaking, refer any single group of people to a fixed task or lot in society on the basis of their nature (which is precisely what he appears to do in the *Politics*), for example women to the household, for he himself has explained that nature is not deterministic in that way. We are born with a definite biological sex (he thinks), but that potentiality can be realized in different ways.[48]

In spite of her assertion to the contrary, however, Nussbaum's description of human nature is not obviously normative

---

[45] Nussbaum, *Aristotle's* De Motu Animalium, pp. 103-104.

[46] Nussbaum, *Aristotle's* De Motu Animalium, p. 106.

[47] See Aristotle, *Metaphysics* IX.5.

[48] This is thus how Nussbaum could answer those who have criticized her rehabilitation of Aristotle's political philosophy, like Knoll, *Aristokratische oder demokratische Gerechtigkeit?*, pp. 222-223, 254, and Richard Mulgan, "Was Aristotle an 'Aristotelian Social Democrat'?", *Ethics* 111:1 (2000), pp. 79-101.

at all, which is probably the reason why she has been charged with a naturalization of morality. In her own words:

> When I imagine a picture of the good or valuable life, and think of wishing it for myself or for another, I ought to get clear about the relationship between that valuable life and the conditions of my (my friend's) continued existence. I ought, that is, to ask closely whether this imagined life is a life that could be lived by such a being as I am – by a being, that is, who shares all those characteristics that I consider to be truly constitutive of my (my friend's) identity.[49]

When phrased in these terms, the question concerning what kind of life is accessible for man looks like an objective question. The impression is strengthened by the fact that Nussbaum's contrast in this connection is Socrates, who in the *Phaedo* welcomes death as the separation, and therewith liberation, of his soul from the body.[50] In Nussbaum's interpretation, Socrates here desires a life without a body, but that is obviously not a human life.[51]

Moreover, Nussbaum's list of capabilities, in terms of which she wants to formulate her normative (and Aristotelian) conception of human nature, mainly looks like a number of basic needs that all human beings have, like the need for food, rest, meaningful relations, being recognized as an individual person, and so on.[52] The question concerning the good life is therewith turned into a political program centered on basic human rights. As to how one actually leads one's life on the basis of these so-called capabilities, is an issue that Nussbaum does not want to enter into, since she thinks this must be a matter of personal choice. In this respect Nussbaum's position obviously differs from Aristotle's

---

[49] Nussbaum, "Aristotle on Human Nature and the Foundations of Ethics", p. 91.
[50] Plato, *Phaedo* 115c-e.
[51] Nussbaum, "Aristotle on Human Nature and the Foundation of Ethics", p. 93.
[52] Nussbaum's most systematic exposition of her capabilities approach is *Women and Human Development: The Capabilities Approach* (Cambridge: Cambridge University Press, 2000).

virtue ethics, as she herself acknowledges.[53] In fact, one may wonder whether anything remains of Aristotle's idea that the human good is the "activity of the soul in conformity with virtue".[54]

But let us return to the question concerning anthropocentrism: if that position entails an ambition to found ethics on an idea about human nature, which however in its turn is thought to be an expression of a normative stance, then the appeal to nature does not seem to matter that much, but "human nature" only represents a more basic level of the ethical realm about which we may hopefully reach agreement. But this line of reasoning just throws us back to the question of how we can argue with and convince those who do not already share our norms. It is above all when agreement is lacking that the difficulty becomes apparent.[55] At this point, the ambiguity of Nussbaum's internalist anthropocentrism becomes particularly apparent. On the one hand, she has emphasized that the point in referring to nature in this context is not to obtain a criterion that enables us to settle ethical disputes without engaging in any ethical judgment of our own, but only to find a basic level of agreement.[56] This is to say that her list of capabilities is not an absolute one, nor is it intended to be a list of external criteria, but it is the expression of an ethical, subjective position which others are free to scrutinize in the light of their own convictions.[57] But on the other hand, she still wants to talk about human nature as a foundation of ethics, assuming, it seems, that it is only in our nature that we can find something that unites us all, as humans, across cultural and other borders. This nature, moreover, sets limits for our moral lives, though not in the way our biological nature does this, since the latter is of no

[53] See Nussbaum, "Human Functioning and Social Justice", p. 225; "Aristotelian Social Democracy", p. 217; "Aristotle, Politics, and Human Capabilities", p. 124.

[54] Aristotle, *Nicomachean Ethics* 1098a16-17.

[55] For a critical assessment of Nussbaum on this point, see Gutschker, *Aristotelische Diskurse*, pp. 434-440.

[56] Nussbaum, "Aristotle, Politics, and Human Capabilities", p. 120.

[57] See Nussbaum, "Aristotelian Social Democracy", p. 219.

ethical consequence. Instead, it must be our nature such as it is lived from within, and this nature, Nussbaum apparently thinks, is intrinsically normative. Nussbaum thus identifies the internal with the normative, which is hardly uncontroversial.[58] In this way, she tries to achieve a delimitation of the scope and nature of ethics from both the inside and the outside as it were, so that "what a being who stands apart from our experiences and ways of life thinks seems to matter little, if at all".[59]

As a consequence, Nussbaum's internalist or anthropocentric position seems, after all, to be a matter of recognizing that we have no option but to navigate within those basic norms within which we all are captured as humans (because that is our nature).[60] But as I see it, the point of internalism, rightly understood, is that the very distinction over against externalism collapses. We do not have to get out of our skins in order to be able to confront something that challenges us, because that kind of friction is a basic ingredient in our subjective experience. This was, by the way, precisely Plato's point: if we search within ourselves, in our own opinions about right and wrong, we will eventually realize that they point toward something else, the ideas, which are not our creation but whose very sense for us lies in them transcending us. It is we who grant to the ideas their status of transcendent measure precisely as we observe how the significance of, for example, the idea of the good can never be exhausted by a single good act. I take the fact that Nussbaum is unable to read Plato in this way as a sign to the effect that she has some problems with transcendence. After all, there are those who have criticized Aristotle's ethics for having given up on the theory of forms, precisely on the basis of the question con-

---

[58] See Nussbaum, "Aristotle on Human Nature and the Foundations of Ethics", pp. 88, 102. See also Antony, "Nature and Norms", p. 20.
[59] Nussbaum, "Aristotle on Human Nature and the Foundations of Ethics", p. 121.
[60] See Nussbaum, "Appendix on the function of man", *Aristotle's* De Motu Animalium, pp. 100-106.

cerning what he has to offer by way of replacement.[61] I think, however, that Aristotle is more or less in agreement with Plato on this point, and one can see this if one turns to the last book of the *Nicomachean Ethics*, which many of Aristotle's adherents, not least Nussbaum, have difficulties with, because here he abandons his focus on the life of action in *polis*, guided by *phronēsis*. If one really has the ability to see what is good for oneself (which is the mark of *phronēsis*), Aristotle remarks, then one will choose the life of contemplation (*bios theōrētikos*), since man is not the best thing in the cosmos (1141a33-b1).[62] Knowing oneself thus involves wanting to transcend oneself, namely, towards the divine and the eternal. Nussbaum is known to quote Aristotle in a misleading way, and on one occasion, when she is looking for support for her view that ethics is about what is specifically human, she cites the last book of the *Nicomachean Ethics*, where Aristotle says that "it would be strange if one were to choose, not one's own life but that of another" (1178a3-4). But what Aristotle is describing as one's own life is exactly that which is dedicated to nurturing what is alien, one's reason, which is the divine element in man. The latter is, thus, both what is most alien and most proper to man; and it is only by pursuing this element that one can become perfect as a human being, even though this life, as Aristotle puts it, strictly speaking is "too much for man" (1177b26-27).

In this respect, Aristotle's ethics is clearly not anthropocentric: it sets out from the human realm, only to find that the human itself is not purely human but contains within itself a tendency toward that which transgresses us, as a more perfect existence which we should to everything to resemble. In this way, Aristotle spells out the implications of Plato's "god's-eye standpoint", to use Nussbaum's expression. To occupy the inter-

---

[61] Franz Dirlmeier, *Aristoteles, Nikomachische Ethik* (Berlin: Akademie Verlag, 1956), p. 284.

[62] For Aristotle's view that the life of contemplation is the best life, see in particular the *Nicomachean Ethics* X.8.

nal position, or to stay within the circle of appearances, is not the same thing as being confined to what is human, nor, for that matter, to the normative realm, as Nussbaum occasionally seems to think. Rather, it is to be able to "reach out" to something that is, somewhat paradoxically, already immanent to us. If anything, human nature is precisely this transcendence.

Martha Nussbaum and Liberal Education

Anders Burman

After her important works on ethics in Greek and Hellenistic philosophy, *The Fragility of Goodness* (1986) and *The Therapy of Desire* (1994), Nussbaum in 1997 published *Cultivating Humanity: A Classical Defense of Reform in Liberal Education*. Like the former books it is replete with references to classical philosophers such as Socrates, Aristotle and Seneca, but it is also based on empirical investigations of how courses are designed at several contemporary American liberal arts colleges.[1] The main argument in *Cultivating Humanity* is that all students, regardless of the direction of their academic education, must be given the opportunity to develop some basic intellectual capacities which Nussbaum perceives as desirable, not to say absolutely necessary, in a well-functioning multicultural, democratic society. She highlights above all three capacities: to be able to critically examine one's own prejudices, to see oneself in others, and to regard oneself as a world citizen.

---

[1] To be able to write this empirical part of the book, which contains many inspiring illustrations of how high-quality education could look like in practice, Nussbaum gathered together informants from fifteen liberal arts colleges who provided reports for her. Along with classical philosophical texts, these reports are the basis for her reflections on how a good higher education should be designed. See Martha Nussbaum, *Cultivating Humanity: A Classical Defense of Reform in Liberal Education* (Cambridge, MA: Harvard University Press, 1997), preface.

The purpose of this article is to introduce, analyze and contextualize Nussbaum's defense of a reform of liberal education in general and these three capacities in particular. In which intellectual context does she formulate her proposal of a reform in liberal education? How does she think that a contemporary liberal arts education should be designed in the best way? Which topics should be studied and which teaching methods should be used? And finally, how does all this relate to Nussbaum's thinking in general, including her later book on the humanities, *Not for Profit*?

Beyond Postmodern Relativism and Cultural Conservatism

Nussbaum's defense of liberal education in *Cultivating Humanity* is mainly directed toward two targets: on the one hand, some postmodern theories, and on the other hand, a kind of cultural and educational conservatism. It is between these two poles that Nussbaum formulates her ideas on liberal education reform.

When Nussbaum published her book in 1997 she regarded postmodernism, associated with French thinkers such as Jean-François Lyotard, Jean Baudrillard and Jacques Derrida, as a main threat to the classical heritage as well as to the enlightenment ideals that she vindicates. She insists that postmodern thinkers oppose any form of objectivity without any convincing argument, and thus objects to what she perceives as their pronounced relativism and criticism of the concept of truth. Regarding the question of truth and objectivity, Nussbaum claims that analytical and linguistically oriented philosophers, such as Donald Davidson, Hilary Putman and Willard Van Quine, are far more insightful than Derrida and other postmodernists. According to Nussbaum, it is significant that these French thinkers' ill-founded theories have not had any real impact on the discipline of philosophy in the United States, but only on other humanistic disciplines such as literature and rhetoric.[2]

Nussbaum is even more critical to the way postmodern ideas have been used by many American academics. She dismisses in particular Judith Butler's theories of gender and performativity. In a thoroughgoing negative review for *The New Republic*, in which Nussbaum deals with several of Butler's books, Nussbaum presents her as typical of the postmodern turn in American feminism. While feminism was formerly associated with concrete women's struggle, Nussbaum argues that, like many other contemporary feminists, under to a lesser and greater degree the influence of Foucault and other French philosophers, Judith Butler is mainly engaged in theoretical questions without any practical political significance. In fact, Butler's theories serve to support an "amoral anarchist politics." It is a feminism that Nussbaum dismisses as confused, almost sophistic and philosophically substandard. "Butler's hip quietism", Nussbaum concludes, is "cooperating with evil", further adding that "Feminism demands more and women deserve better."[3]

Nussbaum's far from sophisticated objections to Derrida, Foucault and Butler are reminiscent of many of the criticisms of postmodernism that were during the same period pronounced by some American conservative intellectuals, including Allan Bloom, Roger Kimball and Dinesh D'Souza. They too turned against what they regarded as the relativistic approach extolled by these theorists, considering them to have undermined the values of the true, good and beautiful as well as—by extension—

---

[2] It can be noted that Nussbaum is not as harsh on Foucault as she is about Derrida. About Foucault's writings, she maintains that there are some insights that make them "the only truly important work" produced "under the banner of 'postmodernism'". Foucault's analysis on the whole is, nevertheless, characterized by "historical incompleteness" and "lack of conceptual clarity." Nussbaum, *Cultivating Humanity*, p. 40.

[3] Martha Nussbaum, "The Professor of Parody", in *Philosophical Interventions: Reviews, 1986–2011* (New York: Oxford University Press, 2012), pp. 198-215; quotes on p. 213 and 215.

the whole Western cultural and educational tradition. They argued moreover, like Nussbaum, that philosophy—especially classical philosophy—should play a far more prominent role in both education and society than is generally the case now.

Bloom, one of the most prominent of these conservative intellectuals advocating a traditionalist anti-postmodernist and anti-relativistic position, was professor of philosophy at the University of Chicago and author of the bestseller *The Closing of the American Mind*, with the telling subtitle *How Higher Education Has Failed Democracy and Impoverished the Souls of Today's Students* from 1987. The book was to be an influential part of the controversy known as the Culture Wars, a highly polarized controversy during the 80s and 90s revolving around a large number of issues—from religion, abortion and sexuality to youth culture, music and the kind of literature students should be studying at colleges and universities; a set of issues that the combatants perceived as addressing the meaning of American identity and its culture. That both the design of higher education and the curriculum offered at liberal arts colleges became such provocative areas of public policy was at least in part due to the fact that its outcomes were thought to have direct implications for which ideals, values and analytical categories would guide future American leaders.[4]

In *The Closing of the American Mind* Bloom criticizes what he regards as a pronounced leftism in contemporary higher education institutions. He maintains that many intellectuals in the wake of the backlash against the radical ideas of 1968 have been strongly affected by Nietzsche's perspectival theories. Bloom sees a similar kind of relativism and nihilism among his students.

---

[4] James Davison Hunter, *Culture Wars: The Struggle to Define America: Making Sense of the Battles over the Family, Art, Education, Law, and Politics* (New York: Basic Books, 1991), p. 211. See also William Casement, *The Great Canon Controversy: The Battle of the Books in Higher Education* (New Brunswick & London: Transaction Publishers, 1996) and Andrew Hartman, *A War for the Soul of America: A History of the Culture Wars* (Chicago: The University of Chicago Press, 2015), pp. 222-252.

The situation is even more problematic due to the current diversification and specialization of higher education. As a counterforce against all these tendencies, Bloom proposes a return to "the good old Great Books approach": what the students should study the classical books of western literature, philosophy and science.[5]

The great books movement, to which Bloom refers, had its most typical and grandiose expression with the *Great Books of the Western World*, which was published in the early 1950s with Mortimer J. Adler and Robert Maynard Hutchins as the main editors. In 54 volumes they republished 443 classical texts— literary as well as philosophical and scientific, from Homer to Freud.[6] During the 70s and 80s this type of canonical thinking, with focus on dead white men (none of the authors in *Great Books of the Western World* were female), was subjected to fierce criticism from not only feminists but also postmodernists and post-colonialists. That the concept of the great books nevertheless was already at the fore when Bloom wrote his book was due to the fact that the *Great Books of the Western World* had just been re-published in a second, expanded edition in 1990. According to Bloom, it is this kind of classical work, from ancient tragedians and philosophers to some of the writers, thinkers and scientists during the 20th century, that students should spend most of their study time reading and discussing. One thing is for sure, he writes: "wherever the Great Books make up a central part of the curriculum, the students are excited and satisfied, feel they are doing something that is independent and fulfilling, getting something from the university they cannot get elsewhere."[7]

---

[5] Allan Bloom, *The Closing of the American Mind: How Higher Education has Failed Democracy and Impoverished the Souls of Today's Students* (New York: Simon and Schuster, 1997), p. 344.
[6] See Tim Lacy, *The Dream of a Democratic Culture: Mortimer J. Adler and the Great Books Idea* (New York: Palgrave Macmillan, 2013) and Daniel Born, "Utopian Civic-Mindedness: Robert Maynard Hutchins, Mortimer Adler, and the Great Books Enterprise", in DeNel Rehberg Sedo (ed.), *Reading Communities from Salons to Cyberspace* (New York: Palgrave MacMillan, 2011).
[7] Bloom, *The Closing of the American Mind*, p. 344.

Although there is much that reconciles Nussbaum and Bloom—not least their idealization of ancient philosophy and struggle against various forms of relativism—she refused his critical view of contemporary academy. In a long review of *The Closing of the American Mind*, published in *The New York Review of Books*, Nussbaum distances herself from Bloom and his critical description of the higher education system. It is simply not true, as the conservative professor maintains, that the American colleges and universities are in a serious crisis, that students are rootless as well as narcissistic or that contemporary academics generally lack both passion and quality. If someone lacks academic quality and probity it is Bloom, Nussbaum emphasizes and shows that his book is filled with inaccuracies and highly questionable interpretations.[8]

The objections that Nussbaum directs against Bloom affect to some extent the whole conception of great books. In *Cultivating Humanity* she writes:

> It is an irony in contemporary "culture wars" that the Greeks are frequently brought onstage as heroes in the "great books" curricula proposed by many conservatives. For there is nothing on which the Greek philosophers were more eloquent, and more unanimous, than the limitations of such curricula.[9]

Although Nussbaum has a strong belief in the educational value of classical books, in contrast to Bloom, she points out that world literature is much larger and richer than what is represented by the European and North American cultural sphere. The curriculum needs thus to be expanded with other perspectives and traditions.

[8] Martha Nussbaum, "Undemocratic Vistas", in *Philosophical Interventions: Reviews, 1986–2011* (New York: Oxford University Press, 2012), pp. 36-52.
[9] Nussbaum, *Cultivating Humanity*, p. 33. In addition to the concept of the great books, Nussbaum denounces Bloom's normative chauvinism and "militant ethnocentrism". Nussbaum, *Cultivating Humanity*, p. 132; "Our Pasts, Ourselves", in *Philosophical Interventions*, p. 89.

Let Us Cultivate our Humanity

With a retrospective view, Nussbaum could state that her review of *The Closing of the American Mind* in 1987 was the starting point for her work with educational theoretical questions that a decade later resulted in *Cultivating Humanity*.[10] The title of the book from 1997 alludes to a quote by Seneca, which also serves as the motto of the book, "while we live, while we are among human beings, let us cultivate our humanity".[11] This classical notion of human cultivation is at the heart of Nussbaum's defense of liberal education. Since every human being is basically political and active, a *zoon politikon*, to borrow the Aristotelian notion, the cultivation of humanity has an intimate connection to citizenship.

The idea of liberal education implies, according to Nussbaum, "a higher education that is a cultivation of the whole human being for the functions of citizenship and life generally".[12] The relationship between liberal education and democratic political life is a topic that during recent decades has attracted much attention in the sphere of educational research, but unlike most others who write about civic education Nussbaum consistently goes back to Aristotle and other ancient thinkers. She emphasizes that the discussion in *Cultivating Humanity* is specifically based on three themes from the Greek and Roman philosophy:

> [O]n Socrates' concept of "the examined life," on Aristotle's notion of reflective citizenship, and above all on Greek and Roman Stoic notions of an education that is "liberal" in that it liberates the mind from the bondage of habit and custom, producing people who can function with sensitivity and alertness as citizens of the whole world.[13]

---

[10] Nussbaum, *Cultivating Humanity*, p. xi.
[11] Nussbaum, *Cultivating Humanity*, p. xiii.
[12] Nussbaum, *Cultivating Humanity*, p. 9.
[13] Nussbaum, *Cultivating Humanity*, p. 8.

These classical ideas are thus the inspiration for Nussbaum's attempt to formulate a modern and democratic conception of liberal education. Socrates' ideas are of importance in terms of the critical thinking and self-reflection which education should promote and which is the first of three capacities specifically highlighted in *Cultivating Humanity*. The other two capacities are the ability to consider oneself as a world citizen and the empathic capacity to place oneself in the position of another person, which Nussbaum in an original way connects to what she calls the narrative imagination.

Critical Thinking and the Examined Life

The first capacity that all higher education should cultivate among the students is, according to Nussbaum, Socratic self-examination and critical thinking. Socrates serves here as the role model, for it was Socrates who, after the earlier philosophers' speculations on nature and cosmos, brought philosophy down to earth and made it to a concern for all people, underlining the importance of everyone to think critically and independently. He even claimed that an unexamined life is not worth living, which Nussbaum reinterprets in the following way: that a life in wonder and thinking "is not just something useful; it is an indispensable part of a worthwhile life for any person and any citizen".[14]

Through the ages it has been discussed whether and in what ways Socrates' thinking may be distinguished from Plato's idealistic philosophy. For Nussbaum it is clear that it is not only possible but necessary to separate them from each other, at least from a political point of view: while Plato was an aristocratic elitist, Socrates was a convinced democrat who argued that the vast majority of the people has at its disposal the sufficient intellectual prerequisites to be good citizens. Nevertheless, as Nussbaum goes onto note, even Socrates' thinking has some limitations when it is judged by contemporary standards. In many

[14] Nussbaum, *Cultivating Humanity*, p. 21.

ways it was Seneca and the stoics who had properly drawn out the pedagogical implications of Socrates' notion on the examined life. Their educational interpretation of the Socratic conception of the good life may according to Nussbaum be summarized in four statements: liberal education is intended for all people; it should be individualized and adapted to students' different circumstances and contexts; it should be pluralistic and treat a variety of norms, ideas and traditions; and books should not be used in an authoritative way. In line with these conditions, Nussbaum advocates a Socratic dialogue-based teaching and is reassured by the fact that this is already the common medium through which education is conducted at many contemporary liberal arts colleges:

> Liberal education in our colleges and universities is, and should be, Socratic, committed to the activation of each student's independent mind and to the production of a community that can genuinely reason together about a problem, not simply trade claims and counterclaims.[15]

Through the Socratic method, students are encouraged to develop their critical thinking. This should be directed not least against their own prejudices and any such beliefs they embrace by virtue of their upbringing without having the possibility of reflecting upon them. Reason must be recognized as the highest intellectual authority, standing above customs as well as traditions of different kinds.

When Nussbaum in this context speaks of a need for philosophy, she does not primarily mean logic or the study of various metaphysical subtleties. What is needed is rather a practical philosophy based on contemporary issues. Philosophical thought arises, generally speaking, in relation to different problems that confront us in our everyday life. It is also in such a way that philosophical education should be designed, which is often the

---

[15] Nussbaum, *Cultivating Humanity*, p. 19.

case at current liberal arts colleges. "Instead of learning logical analysis in a vacuum", Nussbaum writes, "students now learn to dissect the arguments they find in newspapers, to argue about current controversies in medicine and law and sports, to think critically about the foundations of their political and even religious views."[16]

It is this practical and useful philosophy that all students should encounter during their higher education studies. The concrete philosophical courses may be designed in many different ways, but as a starting point they might, for example, take discussions of classical philosophical texts or actual moral dilemmas. Questions and problems of that kind have gradually been placed in greater focus among contemporary American philosophers, Nussbaum says:

> Given the tremendous importance, for citizenship and for life in, of producing students who can think clearly and justify their views, a course or courses in philosophy play a vital role in the undergraduate liberal arts curriculum. If philosophy presents itself as an elite, esoteric discipline preoccupied with formal notations and with questions of little evident human interest, it will not be able to play this role. But professional philosophy has increasingly over the past twenty years, returned to the focus on of basic human interests that it had in the time of John Dewey and William James.[17]

For Nussbaum, it is obvious that philosophy and critical thinking are intimately connected to a democratic and political life. If democracy would not be reduced to "a marketplace of competing interest groups", education has to "foster a democracy that is reflective and deliberative".[18] That young people develop their ability to reason critically over their own prejudices is ultimately good for democratic society. In line with this argumen-

---

[16] Nussbaum, *Cultivating Humanity*, p. 18.
[17] Nussbaum, *Cultivating Humanity*, p. 41f.
[18] Nussbaum, *Cultivating Humanity*, p. 19.

tation, Nussbaum formulates a deliberative vision of a democratic society where politics is ultimately determined by the best arguments based on a variety views and positions. In every democratic society freedom of speech has to be guaranteed and citizens must regularly have the opportunity to have their voices heard in general elections. But it is also important, Nussbaum stresses, that people can in other ways participate in politics as well as providing the younger generation with the opportunities of participating in a broad civic education. For it is at schools and colleges that the foundation is laid for a democratic active life.

Cosmopolitanism

Nussbaum points out that we as human beings do not only belong to the group of our closest or smaller community. Since all of us relate to the world at large, we should as much as possible strive to think of ourselves as citizens in the world. In *Cultivating Humanity* the notion of a cosmopolitan identity is highlighted as the second capacity that all higher education should try to cultivate among its students.

Nussbaum quotes the well-known statement of Diogenes of Sinope, "I am a citizen of the world".[19] This ancient cynic philosopher coined the concept of cosmopolitanism, before the stoics further developed it, turning it into an intellectual and political tradition in its own right. For the stoics, we belong at one and the same time to the community in which we are raised and to mankind at large. In the sense of the latter, we are *kosmopolitēs*. The idea of being a world citizen was an integral part of the stoics' general philosophy, according to which all people are united in common universal reason. In addition, they developed an educational program aimed at making the younger generation aware that they are citizens of the world and that it is better to accept the necessary order of all things. Such a cosmopolitan upbringing and education, Nussbaum says, "requires transcending

---

[19] Nussbaum, *Cultivating Humanity*, p. 52.

the inclination of both students and educators to define themselves primarily in terms of local group loyalties and identities."[20]

At various times throughout history, the cosmopolitan tradition has been revived, for instance, during the Enlightenment by Thomas Paine, Immanuel Kant and other philosophers. When Nussbaum at the end of the 20th century wrote *Cultivating Humanity*, cosmopolitanism was again on the political and philosophical agenda. Thinkers such as Jürgen Habermas, Ulrich Beck and David Held were intensively discussing cosmopolitan theories. Like Nussbaum, most of them may politically be defined as social democrats or left-wing liberals. In addition, they were more or less explicitly committed to capitalize on the best of the cosmopolitan heritage in both antiquity and the Enlightenment. At the same time, they were opposed to conservative interpretations of the current political situation after the Cold War. One of these conservative thinkers was Samuel Huntington, the American political scientist, who in the book *The Clash of Civilizations and the Remaking of World Order* from 1996 claimed that the fall of Soviet communism had led to a new world order where the decisive battle is no longer fought between communism and capitalism, but between different monolithic cultures or civilizations, such as Western, Muslim and Chinese-Confucian.[21]

The theorists of cosmopolitism problematize this simplistic and homogenizing narrative through highlighting what is common to different cultures and the actual forces working for a peaceful cooperation that exist between them. Habermas, for instance, sees the United Nations as the central organization in the efforts to find new forms for a democratic order beyond the traditional nation states.[22] But however laudable this may seem

---

[20] Nussbaum, *Cultivating Humanity*, p. 67.

[21] Samuel Huntington, *The Clash of Civilizations and the Remaking of World Order* (New York: Simon & Schuster, 1996).

[22] See, for instance, Jürgen Habermas, "A Political Constitution for the Pluralist World Society?", in *Between Naturalism and Religion: Philosophical Essays*, trans. Ciaran Cronin (Cambridge, UK: Polity Press, 2008).

from an abstract historical and geopolitical perspective, there is indeed something idealistic with such notions of a future cosmopolitan democratic world order. In today's world there are so many conflicts and opposing interests that cannot be contained in such a cosmopolitan project, and politics in itself may even be said to contain within itself an irresolvable conflict that cannot be reconciled by means of reaching an underlying consensus advanced by leading theorists of cosmopolitism. Indeed, is not politics, as the French philosopher Jacques Rancière underlines, based on dissensus rather than consensus?[23] This, however, is a position that neither Nussbaum nor Habermas countenances.

Although Nussbaum shares many of Habermas' and the other cosmopolitan theorists' basic assumptions and conclusions, she differs from most of them since her primary interest in cosmopolitanism is not because it is a transnational phenomenon.[24] The cosmopolitanism with which *Cultivating Humanity* deals is rather a moral and pedagogical issue, with a focus on how education at liberal arts colleges should be designed. In this context, Nussbaum emphasizes the importance of learning foreign languages and studying non-Western cultures as well as including knowledge of minorities in the curriculum and to undertake systematic work with regard to a fully integrated gender perspective. All of this would accordingly contribute to the development of the students' multicultural and cosmopolitan self-understanding.

The Narrative Imagination

The narrative imagination—the ability to imagine how it would be like to be in someone else's situation—is the last of the three capacities discussed in *Cultivating Humanity*. Nussbaum points out that this ability, which in another context she remarks is

---

[23] Jacques Rancière, "Ten Theses on Politics", in *Dissensus: On Politics and Aesthetics*, trans. Steven Corcoran (London: Bloomsbury Academic, 2016), p. 45.
[24] Marilyn Friedman, "Education for World Citizenship", *Ethics* vol. 110, No. 3, 2000, pp. 586-601.

perhaps the most important of the three capacities,[25] can be improved by reading realistic novels such as Charles Dickens' *Hard Times*, Henry James' *Portrait of a Lady* or Richard Wright's *Native Son*. Based on the novel's narration we may—through our imagination—identify ourselves with different characters. The same is true in our life-world; when we try to understand another person and her actions, we do it best by placing them into a narrative. Through the reading of novels one may thus improve the ability to situate oneself in another person's position and life situation.

In her discussion on the narrative imagination and the role of literature in education Nussbaum refers to Aristotle's notion of the philosophical precedence of poetry over historiography; poetry depicts what might happen in a more logical and generally valid narration instead of what actually has occurred. "This knowledge of possibilities is an especially valuable resource in the political life", Nussbaum writes.[26] Alongside this narrative imagination, she refers to a civic and compassionate imagination as well as a democratic imagination, but without clarifying the relationship between them.[27] Still she emphasizes: "If the literary imagination develops compassion, and if compassion is essential for civic responsibility, then we have good reason to teach works that promote the types of compassionate understanding that we want and need."[28] A genuine liberal education should, then, in a systematic way use various kinds of fiction, especially a certain kind of narrative fiction.

---

[25] Martha Nussbaum, "Political Soul-Making and the Imminent Demise of Liberal Education", *Journal of Social Philosophy* vol. 37, No. 2 2006, p. 309.

[26] Nussbaum, *Cultivating Humanity*, p. 86. Aristotle, *Poetics*, trans. James Hutton (New York: Norton, 1982).

[27] See, e.g., Nussbaum, "Education for Democratic Citizenship". Lecture delivered on the occasion of the awarding of the degree of Doctor Honoris Causa at the Institute of Social Studies, The Hague, The Netherlands, 9 March, 2006; www.iss.nl/fileadmin/ASSETS/iss/Documents/Academic_publications/nussbaum_text.pdf (2018-08-09).

[28] Nussbaum, *Cultivating Humanity*, p. 99.

It seems like Nussbaum in *Cultivating Humanity* prioritizes literature over other art forms and, moreover privileges the realist novel over other literary genres—with the exception of Walt Whitman, whose "democratic poetry" in *The Leaves of Grass* she has a particular fondness for.[29] She claims that the novel defends the "Enlightenment ideal of the equality and dignity of all human life", but not "uncritical traditionalism".[30] According to such a normative perspective one may ask how literature that is neither edifying nor supportive of the elevated ideals of the Enlightenment should be estimated, for example Marquis de Sade's violent erotic fantasies or William Burroughs' hallucinatory *The Naked Lunch*. Although the realistic novel may be an excellent medium for the cultivation of self-critical thought and narrative imagination, the same is true for many other things, including other kinds of literature as well as movies, visiting unfamiliar places, and not to forget, simply conversing with other people. Indeed, there is no reason to reduce the means for cultivating self-critical thought and narrative imagination to a certain kind of novel.

When Nussbaum talks about the transformative power of literature it sometimes sounds like she imagines that the content of a novel by itself can make the reader wiser. She argues, for example, "the genre itself, on account of some general features of its structure, generally constructs empathy and compassion in ways highly relevant to citizenship".[31] But the fact is that the actual reader always reads and interprets a text in her own way, based on her previous experiences, knowledge, expectations and the current situation. At best, the reading is processed into an experience that the reader then may carry with her through her life. It is only when literature is embraced in such an active way

---

[29] Nussbaum, *Cultivating Humanity*, p. 96.
[30] Martha Nussbaum, *Poetic Justice: The Literary Imagination and Public Life* (Boston: Beacon Press, 1995), p. 46.
[31] Nussbaum, *Poetic Justice*, p. 10.

that it functions as a means for the development of compassion, empathy and self-formation.

However, these critical reflections or objections do not imply that *Cultivating Humanity* is lacking in strong arguments for a reformed liberal education in which literature as well as other arts play a central role. Nussbaum's way in treating literature as something that basically deals with what it is to be a human being, and her insistence that by reading novels we can learn important things about ourselves, is indeed appealing. The arts, in the broadest sense of the word, may contribute to the cultivation of judgment and the narrative imagination, which is of great importance not only for our empathy but also for civic, democratic life in general. Nussbaum writes: "The arts cultivate capacities of judgment and sensitivity that can and should be expressed in the choices a citizen does."[32] For good reasons literature and art should thus be treated as integral parts of a liberal education that ultimately aims at revitalizing the whole democratic society. According to Nussbaum, a reform of the education system in line with the proposal presented in *Cultivating Humanity* is of great importance. As she puts it in the end of the book: "It would be catastrophic to become a nation of technically skilled people who have lost the ability to think critically, to examine themselves, and to respect the humanity and diversity of others."[33]

Why Democracy Needs the Humanities

When Nussbaum wrote *Cultivating Humanity*, she thought that the American higher education system was in a fairly good condition. However, over a decade later, when she returned to the issue of higher education, with the *Not for Profit: Why Democracy Needs the Humanities*, no longer was Nussbaum convinced.[34] In the book from 2010 she maintains that liberal education

---

[32] Nussbaum, *Cultivating Humanity*, p. 86.
[33] Nussbaum, *Cultivating Humanity*, p. 300.
[34] Martha Nussbaum, *Not for Profit: Why Democracy Needs the Humanities* (Princeton & Oxford: Princeton University Press, 2010).

aiming at students' personal growth, critical thinking and civic education is seriously threatened.

The most immediate threat to liberal education is, according to *Not for Profit*, neither postmodernism nor cultural conservatism. It comes now instead from an increasingly dominant economic ideology according to which the extent of a child's and adolescent's education in schools does not go beyond the need to learn about computer science and technology, in addition to the basic skills of reading, writing and arithmetic. Only rudimentary knowledge of history, art and literature is required, and even less is taught on values associated with gender, equality and democracy. With the focus squarely and entirely on entrepreneurship, economic benefit and gross national product per capita, everything else is, at best, of secondary importance.

This economic growth paradigm, which facilitates an education for profitmaking, has so far only rarely been fully implemented—as examples, Nussbaum refers to some states in India (Gujarat, Andhra Pradesh)—but it is gaining greater traction in both the United States and other parts of the world. In a certain respect, such a model for economic growth stands behind the successive wave of cuts to the arts in schools as well as in the dismantling of the humanities in general, something we have witnessed as a globalizing phenomenon during recent decades, in favor of technological and other skills that seem to be more useful, at least in short economic terms.

It is against this background that Nussbaum is drawn to speak in quite unsettling terms that we are living in the midst of a worldwide educational crisis which we yet barely even noticed, but which left unrecognized is spreading like a deadly cancer. Based on her belief that a prosperous democracy requires well-oriented, empathic and critical thinking citizens, Nussbaum is genuinely concerned that schools, colleges and universities in our time produce useful human machines rather than citizens. Although this, perhaps, could be desirable from a strictly economic point of view, it is particularly unfortunate from a broader, humanistic perspective. What is ultimately at stake is nothing less than the future of democracy.

When Nussbaum formulates her positive alternative to the economic growth model she distinguishes, as in *Cultivating Humanity*, between different abilities that educational institutions of various types should seek to foster. The list of desirable capabilities is longer in *Not for Profit* than in the previous book. Besides the three capacities that were highlighted there—is to think critically, to go beyond one's own local sympathies and instead become a citizen of the world, and through the narrative imagination realizing what it is like to be in other people's life situations—Nussbaum speaks here of the abilities to think well about political affairs, to recognize all human beings as people with equal rights (regardless of their race, religion, gender and sexuality), to concern for the lives of others, to envision the complexity of human life and to judge political leaders in a critical but well-informed and constructive way. This is what the school system—not only liberal arts colleges—should focus on imparting in the younger generations.

On the basis of a series of thinkers such as Socrates, Jean-Jacques Rousseau, Johann Heinrich Pestalozzi, John Dewey, Maria Montessori and Rabindranath Tagore (the Indian Nobel Laureate in Literature 1913 who was also an important educator and founder of an elementary school as well as a university, Visva-Bharati), in *Not for Profit* Nussbaum presents a list of suggestions on how to concretely work with a democratic education. She outlines an ideal education system from kindergarten to college, with small classes, much teaching time and focus on subjects such as world history, foreign language, religion and cultural studies. She stresses also the importance of argumentation analysis, source criticism and critical thinking. Literature and art occupy a central place in this curriculum, not least due to the training of the narrative imagination. At college level, Nussbaum remains faithful to her liberal education ideals, placing due emphasis on philosophical studies. Ideally, she means, all college students would read at least two semesters of philosophy.

Proceeding in this way Nussbaum tries to be more specific in *Not for Profit* than she had been in *Cultivating Humanity*. Nevertheless, many questions remain unanswered. Still more problematic is perhaps the slippage that occurs in her argumentation between the concepts of human beings and citizens. She seems to think that students through their cultivation of humanity may become not only good citizens, but also better human beings. But, one may ask, who has the right and possibility to say that a particular person is better than another, and what constitutes in this context the criteria for deciding between the good and the bad? Considering the moralistic tone that sometimes breaks through in Nussbaum's prose, such as when she connects Judith Butler's gender theories with "evil", Nussbaum sometimes appears to believe that she herself has the ability to determine which people are better and worse, and which are good or evil. However, this type of discussion leads inevitably in the wrong direction and should in no way be encouraged.

Yet, important insights still remain in both *Cultivating Humanity* and *Not for Profit* about the ways in which higher education may contribute to the formation of enlightened, active citizens. With Nussbaum one may ask why not only schools but also colleges and universities should have the right—or even obligation—to try to cultivate their students. Nussbaum points out that this idea is not nearly as prominent in Europe as it is in the United States: "Students in Europe enter university to study one subject, be it law or medicine or philosophy or history or chemistry or classics. There is no idea, in these curricula, of a core of common studies that is essential to the good life for each and every person."[35] However, Stanley Fish reminds us that the notion of the cultivating mission of higher education is not obvious in the United States either. Arguing against any such claims, Fish in *Save the World On Your Own Time* maintains that university and college teachers, *qua* teachers, should not have any ambi-

[35] Nussbaum, *Cultivating Humanity*, p. 31.

tions other than to introduce relevant knowledge to their students and to teach them key analytical skills. In other words: forget character education, civic education, and everything else with which liberal arts colleges usually try to justify their existence.[36]

Regardless of how one thinks about such critical arguments it is clear that Nussbaum is of a completely different opinion. In contrast to Fish, she believes that we must try to accentuate the dimension of social and civic formation present in all forms of academic studies. As the world actually looks like today—globalized, multicultural, unfair, for many even frightening—and when mankind faces greater ecological and climate-related challenges than ever before, there are strong reasons that students should not only learn technical knowledge but also develop their practical judgment and other abilities that facilitate and enrich their own lives and that may have beneficial effects on democratic life in general. That is at least Nussbaum's firm conviction, from which she formulates her passionate defense of a higher education aiming at cultivation of humanity.

[36] Stanley Fish, *Save the World on Your Own Time* (Oxford: Oxford University Press, 2008).

Cosmopolitanism Begins at Home: Or, On Knowing One's Place

Sharon Rider

This essay concerns Martha Nussbaum's philosophy of education. In *Cultivating Humanity*, Nussbaum describes her liberal democratic educational ideal as an education toward "world citizenship".[1] My aim here is to think through her ideas about cosmopolitan education, in *Cultivating Humanity* and elsewhere, in light of certain aspects of Kant's thought. I will not engage in a discussion of her critique of the Kantian ideal of autonomy, nor examine her later reconsideration of cosmopolitanism. My interest is rather in Nussbaum's notion that there is a set of distinct abilities that need to be cultivated for active participation in a liberal democratic order—abilities which, she thinks, are also necessary for a life worthy of being lived for a human being, one that lives up to the demands required for "human dignity".

Echoing familiar liberal themes that can already be found in the work of John Stuart Mill, Nussbaum stresses especially the general idea that any program for human cultivation must be devised with great care, if a democratic polity and personal liberty are to be at all possible. What is needed, she says, is "critical

---

[1] Martha Nussbaum, *Cultivating Humanity: A Classical Defense of Reform in Liberal Education* (Cambridge: Harvard University Press, 1997).

culture".[2] In what follows, I will focus on the idea of education as the careful cultivation of the capacities that Nussbaum regards as indispensable for a good (fair, just, democratic) society and a good (dignified, fully human) life. More specifically, I will look closely at the relationship assumed between the human capacity for reason and the idea that cosmopolitanism is crucial to its development.

Citing Kant's "political" essays, Nussbaum sees an intimate connection between a liberal or democratic attitude, in politics as well as in one's own life, and "critical thinking", or rational self-examination.[3] But oddly, given that the cultivation of en-

---

[2] See, for instance, Martha Nussbaum, "Toward a Globally Sensitive Patriotism", in *Daedalus* Vol. 137, No. 3, *On Cosmopolitanism* (Summer, 2008), pp. 78-93. Nussbaum argues here, as well as in *Political Emotions* (Cambridge: Harvard University Press, 2013), for the importance of strong sentiment for one's country (patriotism), which she thinks can be aroused and enhanced by a proper education about its history and culture, and thus serve as a starting point for critical reflection. But the kind of education argued for is quite literally at the level of the "general culture" of the country, without consideration of its artificial character: in many, if not most, Western and Northern European countries, "national" language and practices are largely top-down constructions of the nineteenth-century modernization project, intended precisely to replace local traditions, dialects and practices in order to create a feeling of national unity and commitment. Among the consequences was the practical annihilation of local and regional languages and forms of life. The program of education that she proposes would be at best a ratcheting up of that crumbling edifice, which has suffered a comparable assault from globalization. The point that I want to make here, however, is simply that to the extent that Nussbaum sees a need for education about the immediate rather than the geographically or temporally remote, it is on a level that takes little account of the concrete starting point of thought in a specific place and time; further, the value of it, for Nussbaum, is emotional engagement, not as a necessary component of reason. While it should be noted that Nussbaum explicitly states that her views about patriotism have changed since 2008, her lack of interest in the hermeneutic insight into the foundational role of place for thinking is not substantially altered.

[3] See, for example, Martha Nussbaum, "Kant and Cosmopolitanism" and "Patriotism and Cosmopolitanism", in *The Cosmopolitanism Reader*, eds. Garret Wallace Brown & David Held (Cambridge: Polity, 2010). The relevant essays by Kant in the first instance are: Immanuel Kant, "Ideal for a Universal History with a Cosmopolitan Intent" and "Perpetual Peace: A

lightened, rational judgment is central to Nussbaum's educational project, she does not work out the argument for the link between rational thought and a cosmopolitan point of view. Let us begin then by noting what Kant seems to have regarded as what we might call "the cosmopolitan capacity of thought".

Liberal Thinking, Liberal Education

The faculty of learning through the free exchange of ideas and evaluations is summed up, famously, in Kant's three maxims for human understanding formulated in §40 of the *Critique of Judgment*, to wit, the intention and capacity to:

i) Think for yourself;
ii) Put yourself in your thinking in the place of everyone else;
iii) Always think consistently.

These three maxims are, respectively, the maxim of unprejudiced thought, the maxim of enlarged thought, and the maxim of consecutive thought.[4]

Kant explains that reason can never be passive, since passivity belongs to the heteronomy of reason, also called prejudice. According to Kant, the greatest prejudice of all is to see the world and its workings as beyond the grasp of human reason. This picture, Kant says, renders us passive, enslaved by and obligated to the authority of others. A man whose mind has been enlarged, on the other hand, however limited his natural gifts, can be educated to disregard the "subjective private conditions of his own judgment, by which so many others are confined, and reflect upon it from a universal point of view (which he can only determine by placing

Philosophical Sketch", in *Perpetual Peace and Other Essays on Politics, History and Morals*, trans. Ted Humphrey (Indianapolis & Cambridge: Hackett, 1983). In the latter, the reference is to the *Metaphysics of Morals*.
[4] Immanuel Kant, *Critique of Judgement*, trans. J. H. Bernard (New York: Hafner Publishing, 1951).

himself at the standpoint of others)".[5] In short, Enlightenment means being able to see clearly that one has starting points that are, from the point of view of another, contingent, and can reasonably be called into question. The third maxim, viz. that of consecutive thought, "is the most difficult to attain, and can only be achieved through the combination of the both former, and after the constant observance of them has grown into habit." Kant summarizes: "We may say that the 1st of these maxims is the maxim of understanding, the 2nd of judgment, and the 3rd of reason."[6]

Kant thinks that the faculties of the human mind (or, as Nussbaum would say, human capabilities) can be cultivated through the right sort of education. Such a cultivation is first and foremost directed toward the actualization of the human potential for autonomy (self-legislation) in the individual, the community, and, ultimately, the species. In his lectures on education, he argues for an "education of a personal character, a free being, who is able to maintain himself, and to take his proper place in society, keeping at the same time a proper sense of his own individuality."[7] (This is more or less what Nussbaum is driving at in her recurring references to "human dignity".) The point of education, then, is in the first instance to be enlightened, rather than informed; to learn how to think, not what to think. Indeed, toward the end of the *Metaphysics of Morals*, in a section on method in teaching ethics, Kant writes that the core of moral education is to make the student aware that he himself can think.[8]

The point of all of this is that unprejudiced, broadminded and consistent thinking does not arise spontaneously or without effort. It is something that *can* be brought about and fostered, that is, while it cannot be taught as such, it can nonetheless be

[5] Kant, *Critique of Judgement*, §40, p. 137.

[6] Immanuel Kant, *Critique of Judgement*, pp. 135-138.

[7] Immanuel Kant, *Education*, trans. Annette Churton (Ann Arbor: University of Michigan Press, 1960), §31, p. 30.

[8] Immanuel Kant, *The Metaphysical Principles of Virtue, Part II of the Metaphysics of Morals*, trans. James Ellington (Indianapolis & New York: Bobbs-Merill, 1964), §50, p. 146.

learned or developed. This is, or ought to be, the goal of educators and educational programs. In the lectures on education,
Kant goes so far as to say that it is through education, and *only*
through education, the basic scheme of which is cosmopolitan,
that humanity can achieve autonomy. This carefully considered
and well-devised program of cultural development cannot be the
work of a few individuals, but is an accomplishment requiring
the involvement of the "whole human race."[9]

Nussbaum's *Cultivating Humanity* and *Not for Profit* are
attempts at providing such a program, suited for our global,
interconnected but also fragmented way of life.[10] Nussbaum
thinks that she can provide a general framework for the cultivation
of the capacity for responsible action, autonomous judgment and
conscientious decision-making, in public affairs as well as in private life, in matters both theoretical and practical. To the objection that ideals of, say, logical coherence, are white, European,
male and heteronormative, Nussbaum responds:

> We do not respect the humanity of any human being unless we
> assume that person to be capable of understanding the basic
> issues of consistency and validity and the basic forms of in-
> ference. We sell that person short as a human being unless we
> work to make that person's potentiality for logical thought into
> an active reality.[11]

This is reminiscent of Donald Davidson's "Principle of Charity",
the charitableness of which consists in attributing to others the
capacity to reason in such a way as to be amenable to our way of
thinking, that is, in such a way that we could, in principle, under-

[9] Kant, *Education,* pp. 10-11.
[10] Nussbaum, *Cultivating Humanity* and *Not for Profit* (Princeton: Princeton
University Press, 2010). The idea of a cosmopolitan ideal of culture and education is also sketched out in Martha Nussbaum, "Patriotism and Cosmopolitanism", in *The Cosmopolitanism Reader*, Garret Wallace Brown &
David Held (eds.) (Cambridge: Polity, 2010). See also her "Kant and Cosmopolitanism" in the same volume.
[11] *Cultivating Humanity*, p. 38

stand their thoughts and actions and deem them rational or reasonable by our own lights.[12] In this view of charity, reason demands of us that we do our best to assimilate alternative or alien forms of thought into our conceptual apparatus. Nussbaum is quite explicit on this point when she writes: "Our task as citizens of the world, and as educators who prepare people to be citizens of the world", will be to make all human beings like our neighbours.[13] This, in her view, is possible insofar as we are all, through enlargement of our thought and vigilant undoing of preconceived notions through education, potential "world citizens".

Local Culture and World Citizenship

Nussbaum writes: "Above all, education for world citizenship requires transcending the inclination of both students and educators to define themselves primarily in terms of local group loyalties and identities."[14] This sounds reasonable enough, if all that is meant is that each and every one of us can recognize the difference between saying "Germany invaded Poland", and saying, "As a Pole, it is important for me to maintain and propagate the claim that Germany invaded Poland". But Nussbaum seems to want to say something more than simply claiming that we should distinguish between what is good or desirable for our-

---

[12] Of course, Davidson's Principle of Charity is intended to make a purely conceptual point, not one about human dignity: "Since charity is not an option, but a condition of having a workable theory, it is meaningless to suggest that we might fall into massive error by endorsing it. Until we have successfully established a systematic correlation of sentences held true with sentences held true, there are no mistakes to make. Charity is forced on us; - whether we like it or not, if we want to understand others, we must count them right in most matters. If we can produce a theory that reconciles charity and the formal conditions for a theory, we have done all that could be done to ensure communication. Nothing more is possible, and nothing more is needed." See Donald Davidson, "On the Very Idea of a Conceptual Scheme", in *Proceedings and Addresses of the American Philosophical Association*, vol. 47 (1973–1974), pp. 5-20.

[13] Nussbaum, *Cultivating Humanity*, p. 60.

[14] Nussbaum, *Cultivating Humanity*, p. 67.

selves or a certain group or community, on the one hand, and states of affairs which are not amenable to revision by virtue of consideration of such interests, on the other. Rather, she is at great pains to use education as a way of lifting students out of their presumably limited and limiting social and cultural contexts by exposing them to what Max Weber called "uncomfortable facts", things that can only be assimilated in their understanding by widening their horizons of experience.[15] She asserts, "There are no surer sources of disdain than ignorance, and the sense of the inevitable naturalness of one's own way."[16] For this reason, "awareness of cultural difference is essential in order to promote the respect for another that is the essential underpinning of dialogue." A theme throughout the book is the idea that there is a necessary connection, not only between "ignorance" of other cultures, histories and ways of life, on the one hand, and a monolithic, insensitive and hegemonic attitude, on the other; but Nussbaum also infers, ipso facto, that exposure to a broad spectrum of ideas, histories and identities, together with training in discussing, challenging and arguing about them, will lead to a tolerant, respectful and creative atmosphere that encourages intellectual and social advancement, progress and "innovation". (In places she sounds not so much like Kant or Mill as Richard Florida: "a trained imagination is essential for innovation, a key to any healthy economy").[17]

[15] Max Weber, "Science as Vocation," in H. H. Gerth & C. Wright Mills (eds.), *From Max Weber* (New York: Oxford University Press, 1958), pp. 129-156.
[16] Nussbaum, *Cultivating Humanity*, p. 68.
[17] Preface to the 2016 Edition of *Not for Profit*, p. xvii. See also p. 10 in the same book. Richard Florida is an influential urban studies theorist whose name came to popular attention at the turn of the last century with *The Rise of the Creative Class and How It's Transforming Work, Leisure and Everyday Life* (New York: Basic Books, 2002), *The Flight of the Creative Class: The New Global Competition for Talent* (New York: Harper Collins, 2005) and *Cities and the Creative Class* (New York: Routledge, 2005). He has since revised his views. See *The New Urban Crisis: How Our Cities Are Increasing Inequality, Deepening Segregation, and Failing the Middle Class—and What We Can Do About It* (New York: Basic Books, 2017).

Herein lies a perplexing and recurring feature of Nussbaum's argumentation in her plea for education as the high road toward enhanced cultural sensitivity. On the one hand, she often refers to the need to break out of the bubble of one's own upbringing, one's native language, community traditions and parochial concerns, etc. On the other, these tend to be described in the most general ideal-typical terms: "Western", "heterosexual", "white", "Christian", and so forth. But these kinds of "identities" are arguably constructed for and within the realm of the political.[18] At the same time, Nussbaum's own manner of arguing sometimes gives the impression of performative inconsistency. Here we have someone who is obviously extremely educated and erudite, cultivated, cosmopolitan. Yet she displays "the sense of the inevitable naturalness of one's own way" that she elsewhere equates, quite emphatically, with egoism and even narcissism: traits that she claims adequate education will dissipate and, ultimately, eradicate.

Nussbaum does not pay much attention to the thought that perhaps it is not possible to revise, amend, enhance or cultivate an education that has been so fragmented as to fail to constitute a genuine identity or culture. The problem for many "white, Christian Western males", for instance, is not that they are too embedded in their own language, local traditions and regional culture, but that they are not embedded at all. They do not know why water comes out of the tap in the kitchen, or what can be grown and cannot be grown given the weather conditions and soil type in the area in which they live; they are unaware of the labours involved when their grandparents first learned to speak English, and they are as a rule clueless as to what decisions were made on what bases and by whom when their hometown was recognized as a municipality; they have not the foggiest idea about the theological differences between their own Baptist up-

---

[18] An account to this effect is offered by bell hooks' observations about the production of white supremacy in rural Kentucky. See bell hooks, *Belonging: A Culture of Place* (London & New York: Taylor and Francis, 2009).

bringing and the practices and beliefs of their Anabaptist neighbours next door. They are, as it were, "culturally disinherited"; they have lost the cultural capital of self-sufficiency that is so important for Nussbaum in her appropriation of Rousseau, and this, among other things, because schooling has taken so little of genuinely local conditions and practices into account. "Place" has, as it were, no place in higher education. It is difficult to see how you will negotiate your way in foreign territory if you do not know where you are to begin with. "Europe" is not a place; it is an idea. A place has a particular climate, specific material and social conditions, distinct forms of interaction and patterns of behavior, often its own dialect and idioms. The liberal world-citizen envisaged by Nussbaum has to start from somewhere. Nussbaum nods distractedly in acknowledgement of this fact, but she does not seem to take its implications seriously as worthy of consideration. A sure sign of this is that the examples she offers of "local" grounding are "American History" and "Anglo-American literature". It is as if Nussbaum thinks that such categories correspond to something real, that there is a unified, "Western, white European culture" that can be "learned". She derides 19th and early 20th century commentators on Aristotle for refusing "to consider that there might be plausible views other than those their philosophical culture was currently discussing. They assumed that theirs was the best philosophical culture, and that everything meaningful about ethical matters was already articulated in it".[19] One might argue that i) Nussbaum is correct in this assessment; ii) she herself demonstrates just how difficult it is to avoid this faux pas.

Similarly, while Nussbaum notes repeatedly that "real cultures have varied domains of thought and activity", this point is made only to address the problem that "non-western" cultures are too often studied with a focus on "an urban elite, ignoring

---

[19] Nussbaum, *Cultivating Humanity*, p. 119.

daily life and the lives of rural people".[20] But nowhere in these books is this problem illustrated with reference, say, to the implementation of EU-policy on crop rotation in rural Sweden and its effects on local social and economic practices.

Finally, Nussbaum seems to think that theorizing about tolerance and conceptions of productive activity from an anthropological point of view instils understanding on a par with actually *having to be* tolerant due to one's living environment, or *having to* work under particular conditions, not for a summer as part of an educational experience, but as an everyday fact of life. For Nussbaum, liberal education (i.e. the production of "truly free and self-governing citizens") is something that can be accomplished through planning and reforms formulated by those who have already to a high degree "achieved" their humanity, who are already "citizens of the world". She writes: "There is a common human tendency to think of one's own habits and ways as best for all persons in all times."[21] Indeed.

Nussbaum is surely right when she insists that human beings as a rule do not flourish if we think only about how we can provide ourselves and our families with bread and a roof over our heads, but not about why we live as we do, and what makes our lives worth living. What is less self-evident is why she thinks that "the humanities are essential to address these questions."[22] Perhaps the humanities can, even should, provide a resource for culture in our day. They are, at best, a contributing factor to, and most of all, an expression of, human dignity. That does not make them a pre-requisite for a properly human life or the use of reason. They can do some good, and it is hard to see how today, in the grander scheme of themes, they can do much harm. But to suggest that knowledge of ancient Greek, acquaintance with the role of the trickster in contemporary Latino novels or appreciation of raga in traditional Indian music are somehow indispen-

---

[20] Nussbaum, *Cultivating Humanity*, p. 128.

[21] Nussbaum, *Cultivating Humanity*, p. 156.

[22] See, for instance, p. 172 in *Cultivating Humanity*.

sable for a form of life conducive to moral or cognitive development is perhaps not the expression high-minded, self-scrutinizing magnanimity that Nussbaum takes it to be. To begin with, it seems to suggest that nothing is to be gained for young Americans or Western Europeans by looking around their own corner, unless that corner happens to be Harvard Square or the Latin Quarter. Rootedness is defined as a problem, rather than a possible solution. Our own specific place in the world, our home, has nothing to teach us about ourselves or others; rather, it is defined as inherently parochial, provincial, confined and confining. This starting point is not merely a worry because it seems to stack the deck in favour of urban intellectuals; the problem is that this predilection reiterates the very kind of thinking that on Nussbaum's own account is profoundly illiberal: the idea that certain kinds of lived experience need not be taken into account. Nussbaum's proposal for the best way to counter the critique of the liberal ideal of world citizenship as a "subtraction story", i.e. what you have left when local, religious, cultural and linguistic factors are removed, would seem to be to replace it with an "addition story", an ideal of the world citizen as within herself "containing multitudes". The deeper issue, however, is that thinking always and of necessity arises somewhere: a thought is a specific orientation in a world. Knowing the conditions of that orientation would be the first step toward seeing it in its specificity and therewith grasping the possibility of other perspectives. "European" or "North American", "male" or "heterosexual" are far too broad characterizations to locate the conditions of one's thinking, however many speeches of Lincoln or Martin Luther King one is exposed to at college.

As an example of an alternative notion of enlarged thinking, one might consider Timothy Larsen's *The Slain God: Anthropologists and the Christian Faith*, where it is argued that the canonical anthropologists E. E. Evans-Pritchard and Mary Douglas were profoundly influenced by their personal experiences of the

Catholic faith and their own religiosity.[23] On Larsen's account, their capacity to recognize the rationality of tribal cultural practices, to understand the nature of ritual from the point of view of a believer, to see the value of hierarchy as an ordering structure, and to acknowledge the centrality of spiritual concerns in cultural systems were directly related to their immersion in Christianity and the Church. In short, it was the richness of their self-understanding that enabled their openness toward other cultures. This requirement that self-knowledge begins at home, i.e. *within* a tradition, receives little attention from Nussbaum, who seems to think that we understand ourselves first when encountering the Other and seeing ourselves with her eyes. One might also object that encounters between distant societies, alternate forms of life, religious beliefs, etc. are portrayed here primarily as a means to enhance self-awareness among white, middle-class American college students.

The clue is how Nussbaum understands "openness", that is, in good liberal fashion as cosmopolitanism in the cultural sense, rather than the philosophical sense. For Nussbaum, a cosmopolitan is at ease with people, artefacts and practices from many countries and cultures, as in phrases such as "her knowledge of French, German, Hindi and Latin made her genuinely cosmopolitan"; or "an influx of students and faculty from around the globe has transformed Euphoria State University into a cosmopolitan hub of international intellectual exchange"; or associated with travel and novel experiences, as in "our research program has collaborations with groups in numerous countries, and is on the cutting edge of the latest global developments." The idea here is that higher education and science are by their nature universal. This is essentially correct. The university has since its inception been relatively "open" in comparison to other institutions at the time, in the sense that joining the community of students and

[23] Timothy Larsen, *The Slain God: Anthropologists and the Christian Faith* (Oxford: Oxford University Press, 2014).

scholars was thought to free its members from the shackles of linguistic parochialism, clan loyalties and provincial prejudices. And universities today indeed stress the value of "openness", "tolerance" and "dialogue".

There seems to be a supposition that we either learn to be liberal cosmopolitans, or we are left in the dark cellar of irrational bigotry and narrow-minded dogmatism. *Heimat und Volk, Blut und Boden.* But to argue that human beings and their institutions, including universities, have a definite place is merely to say that they are real, not virtual. They are actualized in the activities and aspirations of people, who are themselves always somewhere. We all have parents and histories; we are not mushrooms sprung from spores spread by the winds. To know our place is to know who we are, and it is a precondition for grasping the alien and engaging in reasoned dialogue with others. The dissemination of cosmopolitan cultural capital to the benighted masses is in essence the replacement of local doxa with the code of the salon, on the assumption that the latter has achieved a higher state of moral perfection than the former. But according to what criterion? The tolerance and openness advanced by Nussbaum is redolent of the principle of noblesse oblige. But as is often the case when privilege speaks, the public is not invited to participate on an equal footing in the conversation.[24]

Now Nussbaum does emphasize that a truly broadened perspective must be found also in more intimate contexts. Internationalization and a global point of view are not things that can be attained merely at the level of policy and politics, but must be an ongoing, daily effort on the part of individuals and institutions. We must open ourselves to the world by enlarging our

---

[24] I try to untangle precepts of an alternative ideal of education, inspired by Hannah Arendt's reading of Kant, in Sharon Rider, "Coercion by Necessity or Comprehensive Responsibility: Hannah Arendt on Vulnerability, Freedom and Education", in Véronique Fóti & Pavlos Kontos (eds.), *Phenomenology and the Primacy of the Political* (Cham: Springer International Publishing, 2017).

cognitive and moral capacities, which, in turn, requires that we meet with people different from ourselves, who speak other languages and whose beliefs and ordinary assumptions are unlike our own. Such meetings can, of course, lead to toleration and sympathy, but can just as easily lead to conflict and dissolution. The question is what in the enriched program of study she envisions guarantees the effects sought, and how does it achieve this? It is worth considering that while "globalization" tends to be associated primarily with the free market, and "internationalism" with socialist ideals, "cosmopolitanism" is thought to be somehow "above" or "beyond" the fray of current political agendas. It has its beginnings in Enlightenment thinking, for which it connoted the liberation of the individual from religious and political authority, as well as from the biased grasp of the world that loyalty to one's own group or culture can entail. To be "cosmopolitan", for someone like Kant, it will be recalled, was to be capable of impartiality in one's judgments and universality in one's reason. What a higher education can do for students is offer an intellectual experience that makes them think: actively, without prejudice and consistently. They are to be led to see that they have assumptions and that these can be examined critically, without being told by a higher authority what ideas they should or should not embrace. Confrontation with alien thought (which can be everything from the intricacies of tax law in the EU to non-Euclidean geometry to Farsi syntax) means learning how to deal with the cognitive challenges posed by difficult tasks and texts. Why then, does Nussbaum insist so much on exposure to ethnic, gender, religious and cultural diversity as key to cognitive and moral development?

At Home with Reason

Nussbaum wants to see her ideal of cosmopolitan culture and education as, among other things, a way to theorize and complete Rawls' "well-ordered" society so that it can be genuinely stable over time for emotional and ideological collectives.[25] The Kantian Rawls thought that equal respect for citizens requires that a polity not build its political principles on any particular "comprehensive doctrine" of the meaning and basis of life, religious or secular.[26] Political principles ought to be potential objects of "overlapping consensus" among "reasonable citizens", which is to say, those who are respectful of their fellow citizens as equals, and prepared to accept fair terms of cooperation. The principles, which are fairly bare-bones, should be assimilable into the comprehensive doctrines of all citizens. Like a "part" or "model", they can be endorsed at the same time as the citizen endorses the rest of his or her comprehensive doctrine. Consensus becomes a regulative ideal, or even a plausible possibility for the future.

For Rawls, in order to have this function, political principles must be i) narrow in scope; ii) shallow in depth. That is: i) they should avoid controversial metaphysical, religious and even ethical precepts, except insofar as the latter directly involve citizenship entitlements; and ii) they should not be grounded in any controversial metaphysical, religious or ethical claims, i.e. they should be independent of any and all comprehensive schemes regarding knowledge or values. Liberal political principles will build on just those ethical notions that are at their core: equal respect for persons and the correlative idea of human dignity. The principles are not devoid of moral content, which is to say that they are not *purely* procedural and formal. The aspiration is to form a basis for acceptance over time of moral ideals for all citizens, whatever their religious or metaphysical convictions. Even if the citizens should have problems with the political principles (internal strife), the only requirement is that the principles are respectful toward all citizens equally (they establish no doctrine). The implications, of course, have substance: they

---

[25] See John Rawls' *A Theory of Justice* (Cambridge: Harvard University Press, 1971) and *Political Liberalism* (New York: Columbia University Press, 1986).
[26] Martha Nussbaum, *Political Emotions: Why Love Matters for Justice* (Cambridge & London: Harvard University Press, 2013), p. 128.

affect public ceremonies, what is taught in schools, what receives public funding, and so forth.

Nussbaum points to the fundamental flaw in Rawls' model: it leaves out everything that people really care about, what they are prepared to live and die for. So she asks: what are the emotional elements necessary to maintain a liberal society such as that advanced by Rawls? (It will be recalled that, for Nussbaum, emotions are evaluations of a kind, specifically, value judgments, which means that they can be assessed according to the criteria by which we assess other judgments, i.e. rational criteria.) Her aim is to educate not only people's minds, but also their hearts, since, as she says, "Love matters for justice", and the goal is to build a society that is "both rational and just."[27]

The appeal to emotions, often in Nussbaum undergirded by appeals to experimental psychology, is intended to show that there is some blood running through the veins of liberal democratic principles. At the same time, the appeal to emotions and cultures is often in lieu of what is really at stake. Regarding the dilemma of religious institutions of higher learning, Nussbaum writes: "These institutions have a dual mission: advancing higher education in a pluralistic democracy, and perpetuating their specific traditions."[28] This is surely right, but notice that "traditions" here cover what Rawls calls "comprehensive doctrines". It is not clear that such doctrines, taken as "traditions", are the same as the scaffolding on which truth claims rest, the bedrock on which my spade turns. In short, there is nothing that precludes, say, Pietist "unprejudiced, enlarged, or consecutive thought", not as a "tradition" or "heritage", in the sense of an assemblage of artefacts, rituals and canon, but as a *way of life*. That Nussbaum sees education and "traditions" as unrelated, perhaps even in conflict, has to do with specific forms of "comprehensive doctrines", namely,

---

[27] Nussbaum, *Cultivating Humanity*, p. 221.
[28] Nussbaum, *Cultivating Humanity*, p. 258.

those forms that require political manifestation for their realization (fundamentalist religious ideology).

One might want to object here to the implicit equation of liberalism with democracy, that is, the assumption that popular rule without liberal principles guiding it, is not "genuine" democracy, but mere "populism". The issue at stake does not have to do with education, Enlightenment, or experience, but of a "comprehensive doctrine" that holds that only *liberal* democracy is democracy; only *liberal* education is education; only *liberal* reason is rational. A more telling title for *Cultivating Humanity* might have been *Cultivating Good Liberal Democrats*. But if Nussbaum has higher ambitions and deeper aims than preaching for the choir or writing handbooks for likeminded colleagues and policymakers, then she should be prepared to consider more seriously the consequences of the insight that human dignity is in the eyes of the beholder, that there can be other "dignified", indeed rational, forms of life than that of a worldly sophisticate.

A more philosophical ideal of cosmopolitan education would take its bearings from Kant's third Critique, i.e. the ideal that education means training in a rigorous kind of self-discipline in which the student is consistently challenged to think and think again. The first step is to get her to doubt: to see that she does not know very well what she takes herself to know intimately (for instance, her native language), and make her hungry to know more. The second is to force her to articulate what she might know very well (her local surroundings, for instance) in such a way as to make her knowledge communicable and comprehensible to others and explicit to herself. Finally, she should submit herself to the demands of coherence. As Kant points out in a footnote, even if Enlightenment might seem to be quite a simple matter, in practice it is very difficult to accomplish; it is both arduous and slow.[29] Not to allow one's reason to remain passive, but to attain and maintain self-legislation is something

---

[29] Kant, *Critique of Judgement*, p. §40, p. 137, footnote 32.

that is often accompanied by the desire to move beyond what is strictly speaking possible to know, and, importantly, there is no dearth of self-appointed authorities who will satisfy that desire. The most demanding part of enlightenment is to acknowledge that its constitution is only "negative". Its essence is self-regulation and self-correction, nothing more. For this, it requires confrontation with a world of other minds and other thoughts, as well as laws of nature. This encounter ought to begin with what is so immediate that it is barely noticed, like the air we breathe. It is unlikely that Plato know any other language than his mother tongue, yet we have inherited the idea of an Idea, general principles apart from any particular group or collective holding them, from him. And Kant, famously, never left Königsberg.

Capabilities and Human Dignity: On Martha Nussbaum's Understanding of Justice and Human Rights

Jenny Ehnberg

The question of what constitutes justice is perennial for ethics. It has a long pedigree and holds central place also in legal and political philosophy. Of course, the question of justice is vast, and attempting an answer will demand attending to a number of different queries: to whom or what do we owe justice, that is, with which persons, groups or agents, do we stand in relations that should be evaluated in terms of justice; is justice primarily a question of a just and right distribution of resources, or is it recognition and the possibilities for participation in society that different groups have that is the relevant focus of justice theorizing; and what bases for solidarity and justice among persons and nations are there?

Theories focusing on allocation, so-called distributive theories, come in a number of variants. Some argue that the question of justice is primarily a question of establishing what counts as adequate living conditions for all individuals and make sure that these are met. Others maintain that justice requires more far-reaching measures; egalitarians, for instance, claim that justice demands an equal division of resources. Yet these distributive models have been criticized for paying insufficient attention to the structures within which human beings live their lives. Institutions, it is argued, ought also to be included in our conception of justice since they shape society and the structures that situate people in different, and unjust, ways. An important question thus arises: should our understanding of justice formulate a notion of just procedures or should it instead focus on the outcome of a particular distribution or structure? Should a model of justice before all else establish a level playing field upon which people can pursue happiness to the best of their abilities, or should our understanding of justice instead set its sights upon the lives which people are actually able to live, and create a fair outcome for everyone?[1]

Martha Nussbaum has made an important contribution to this debate with her *capabilities approach*, the core of which comprises a list of ten central human capabilities. Developed together with Amartya Sen, the notion of capabilities has had a considerable impact in both academic and practical contexts. Among other things, it has provided inspiration to those working under the aegis of the United Nations, offering a challenge to the focus on economics which has long dominated thinking about development. Its central argument is that poverty must be understood in terms of a lack of human capabilities and that development accordingly requires their expansion.

Current for several years now, Nussbaum's capabilities approach has had a big impact both within and outside the academic world. Only rarely, however, has the conception of justice to which it gives expression been related to ongoing discussions of theories of human rights. Nussbaum has herself noted similarities between her concept and certain formulations of human rights, arguing that there are good reasons to choose her list of core human capabilities in place of the various catalogues of rights which have been developed within the joint framework of the UN.

---

[1] For a thorough investigation into the many varieties of articulations of social justice, and a constructive proposal for a model of justice, see Per Sundman, *Egalitarian Liberalism Revisited: On the Meaning and Justification of Social Justice* (Uppsala: Acta Universitatis Upsaliensis, 2016).

In this article I examine the precise model of justice offered by Nussbaum. I will discuss what is meant by the term "capabilities" and how it relates to the idea of a life that is truly human. I will also address the political role of the list and how exactly Nussbaum regards it as a potential model for social justice. The connection between capability and human rights will also be discussed, after which I will consider the rationale for Nussbaum's view that a list of core human capabilities is justifiable. By way of conclusion, I will address what I see as the advantages of Nussbaum's formulation of the capabilities approach while highlighting a number of critical objections.

Capabilities Approach: A Brief Outline

The capabilities approach has been developed by Indian economist and philosopher Amartya Sen and by Martha Nussbaum. While their expositions of the approach differ on a number of counts, they share the view that justice is dependent on the real life-opportunities which people have to function in certain meaningful ways.[2] The capabilities approach proceeds from the notion of human capability as well as, in Nussbaum's version, the idea that we can identify particular "areas" of human life where we can agree that a lack of capability constitutes a violation of human dignity. According to both Nussbaum and Sen, capabilities are a category of substantial freedoms that enable certain desirable functions in human beings. Nussbaum has proposed a list of ten core human capabilities on the basis of a conception of what constitutes truly human functioning.[3] She describes the list as a philosophical approach that can provide the underpinnings for political guarantees in the form of fundamental rights in every nation in the world. Although the capab-

---

[2] See Martha Nussbaum, *Women and Human Development: The Capabilites Approach* (Cambridge: Cambridge University Press, 2001), p. 71 and Amartya Sen, *The Idea of Justice* (Cambridge: Belknap Press of Harvard University Press, 2009), p. 235.
[3] Nussbaum, *Women and Human Development*, pp. 11f.

ilities included on the list are thus intended to have global applicability, Nussbaum contends that they leave some space for variation in how they are concretized, politically and legally, in different countries. The capabilities included on Nussbaum's list are: life; bodily health; bodily integrity; sense, imagination, and thought; emotions; practical reason; affiliation; other species; play; and control over one's environment (in both a political and a material way).[4]

Nussbaum has connected the issue of capability justice to several practical areas—areas she regards as having too often been excluded from discussions of social justice—and has examined justice in relation to family, religion, people with severe physical and mental impairments and disabilities,[5] non-human species, and international justice, among others.

The Notion of the Dignified Life and Human Capabilities

According to Nussbaum, her list of capabilities is based upon a Marxist-Aristotelian conception of human dignity as defined in terms of truly human functioning. On this view, we are able to recognize when individuals are forced by necessity to behave in a way that is beneath their dignity as human beings. The example she takes up from Marx is of how a starving person treats food. Desperation reduces the starving person to behave in an entirely animal-like fashion. Hunger compels them to fall upon their

[4] The list has remained the same since its first articulation in *Women and Human Development* to her latest book on capabilities, *Creating Capabilities: The Human Development Approach* (Cambridge, MA: Belknap Press of Harvard University Press, 2011). The list in its entirety can be found in Nussbaum, *Women and Human Development*, p. 78.

[5] Nussbaum mostly uses the term "people with impairments and disabilities" to denote persons who have been left out of mainstream discussions on social justice. Nussbaum does, however, argue that what is considered to constitute an "impairment" or a "disability" is to a large extent dependent on social and political structures, since they can either hinder or enable persons to participate in society, see Martha Nussbaum, *Frontiers of Justice: Disability, Nationality, Species Membership* (Cambridge, MA: Harvard University Press, 2006), pp. 14-18, 113f.

food in a way that bears no relation to how humans normally eat, such as planning a meal and sharing it with others. We likewise experience distress when people are treated in a sub-human fashion. On this basis we can conclude that there are modes of existence that we would be unwilling to describe as truly human, which is to say, as worthy of human beings. At this point we encounter the notion of thresholds. Nussbaum contends that there exists a level or threshold to which every person's life and functioning must attain in order for us to be able to call it dignified.[6]

Nussbaum thus invokes Aristotle's idea of truly human function and argues that we can specify certain fundamental capabilities as necessary for human beings to be able to function in a truly human way. When describing the meaning of capability, Nussbaum contends that we ought to understand it as a kind of readiness or potential to function in particular ways that are characteristically human. The capabilities approach thus proceeds from a conception of what it means to function in a truly human way, and, according to Nussbaum, the capabilities on her list specify those conditions which must be met in order for human beings to have the opportunity of functioning in ways that are central to or constitutive of human life.

Nussbaum holds that her paradigm makes a crucial distinction between capability and actual functioning, a distinction that is necessary since it would be an illegitimate constraint upon people's freedom of choice if her list demanded that they function in a particular way. Instead, the notion of core human capabilities establishes a kind of minimum of what all human beings should be guaranteed by way of material, social, and political conditions, after which they themselves are free to choose whether or not they wish to pursue a particular function. In so doing, Nussbaum claims that her list is a form of political liberalism respectful of pluralism.

[6] Nussbaum, *Women and Human Development*, p. 72.

An essential precondition of the list, according to Nussbaum, is the view that people are free and dignified beings who use their reason to lead lives in a relation of mutuality with others. Practical reason, she insists, plays a central role in the notion of truly human functioning because a dignified life requires us to actively use our reason to shape that life, rather than merely following, and thus being shaped by, others. Nussbaum argues that we can recognize this notion in the narratives and life stories of other cultures. For instance, she claims that because we feel distress when someone is treated as being incapable of determining their own life, we can identify a kind of human dignity that transcends context.[7]

But exactly what kind of notion of human dignity is Nussbaum presenting? She states that her conception of human value is Aristotelian rather than Kantian.[8] Dignity involves both our rationality and our bodily existence, and any conception of human dignity must acknowledge both these qualities of human life. For Nussbaum, this point is of particular importance because classical theories of justice, which proceed from the fact that we are rational beings who seek to cooperate with others for our own personal benefit, have excluded people with severe impairments and disabilities. Rather, Nussbaum contends, we should be emphasizing the fact that we are social beings who depend on others in order to be able to lead good lives. We should challenge the idea that we are independent "parties to a contract", roughly equal in strength, upon which theories of the social contract are predicated.[9]

[7] Nussbaum, *Women and Human Development*, pp. 82f.

[8] Nussbaum, *Frontiers of Justice*, pp. 159f.

[9] This is one of the central arguments in *Frontiers of Justice*, where Nussbaum claims that so called "contract theories", that is, theories which proceed from the idea that societal norms and principles should be understood as founded by a "social contract", are unable to include persons with severe impairments and related disabilities (especially mental impairments related to developmental disabilities), non-human animals and relations between different countries in considerations of justice. This is so, she argues, because they proceed from a view of "the contracting parties" as free, independent, and roughly equal in strength. They therefore exclude all relations between

According to Nussbaum, we should in the first instance under-stand the capabilities on the list as preconditions for a dignified human life. Those capabilities, which derive from the notion of truly human functioning, thus represent a set of criteria for what constitutes a dignified human life and what the latter requires by way of political and social protections. Human dignity, argues Nussbaum, should therefore be understood not as a freestanding principle but as part of a vision of the truly human life.[10]

Nussbaum states that her model is explicitly feminist in that it postulates the value and dignity of every human being, and her list identifies capabilities that should be present in every person's life. The lack of recognition of equal value arguably confronts women with particular force in traditional social environments, where they are often reduced to being a part of the "organic unity" of the family. For this reason, our political goal should be to ensure that every individual has a fundamental level of cap-ability within all of the areas of life identified by the list.[11] At the same time, argues Nussbaum, her model proceeds from a notion of equal dignity but not one of equal distribution. In other words, her idea is that we should respect the equal dignity of all human beings by guaranteeing that each of them can live a dig-nified life, but without according the idea of equal human dig-nity an egalitarian significance in the form of a principle of equal distribution.[12]

In her early thinking on capabilities and human functioning, Nussbaum explicitly articulated a kind of essentialism in which the notion of capability was directly connected to an Aristotelian

parties, whether they are persons, non-human animals, or nations, which cannot be described according to this idea of "equality in powers", from considerations of justice. Nussbaum, *Frontiers of Justice*, pp. 25ff., for dis-cussion on the problem of doing justice to persons with severe mental im-pairments, see pp. 98-102.

[10] Nussbaum, *Frontiers of Justice*, p. 162.

[11] Nussbaum, *Women and Human Development*, pp. 84ff.

[12] Nussbaum, *Frontiers of Justice*, p. 295.

conception of human functioning.[13] Nussbaum has subsequently revised her position and now claims that capabilities should not be seen as the timeless expression of a truly human essence but as articulations of what the good life requires under the conditions of modernity.[14] Although Nussbaum can now be said to advocate a modified form of Aristotelianism, she is manifestly ambivalent about whether the view of human beings, or philosophical anthropology, which underpins her model gives expression to a conception of a truly human essence. On the one hand, as has already been noted, her list is said to express a non-perfectionist and pluralistic understanding of human functioning, in which the good life can take many different concrete forms; on the other, she refers to human personality as having a structure that in some measure is independent of context, and to how human beings around the world are united in the fact of bodily existence.[15]

Social Justice and Human Rights

As we have seen, Nussbaum emphasizes the fact that the legitimate political goal is capability and not actual function. It is important, Nussbaum argues, that we understand the difference between capability-deprivation on the one hand, and, on the other, forgoing a specific function. One or more functions may be noticeably absent from a person's life yet this does not constitute injustice when that person has had the opportunity to exercise a particular function but has chosen not to; injustice is, rather, when the capability relating to that function has been absent from the start. For Nussbaum, a model of justice must ensure that all citizens are guaranteed each of the capabilities on

---

[13] Martha Nussbaum, "Human Function and Social Justice: In Defense of Aristotelian Essentialism", *Political Theory*, Vol. 20, No 2, 1992, pp. 202-246, especially pp. 214-223.
[14] Nussbaum, *Women and Human Development*, pp. 78f., 81.
[15] Nussbaum, *Women and Human Development*, pp. 22f., 155.

the list while not requiring of people that they function in a particular way.[16]

Nussbaum holds that her capabilities approach has advantages over those models of justice which focus on the allocation of resources. Since individuals have to function under such widely varying conditions, it is misleading to focus on resources. In order that everyone should attain the "threshold" which underpins the concept of capability, it is necessary that we distribute resources in an unequal way. In order that everyone should be able to function in a truly human way, distribution must acknowledge the conditions and needs which different people have. It is for Nussbaum a matter of creating the conditions, economic as well as social, according to which people might live their lives and find it genuinely possible to satisfy the functions listed. She describes the capabilities on the list as composite or combined capabilities in that it takes different kinds of measures and support for the function in question to be developed. For instance, there is a difference between those functions which are more or less "ready" from birth, such as sight, and those functions which require more support from one's environment in order to develop, such as being able to participate in the political governance of society. It is the latter kind of capabilities that are included in the list.[17]

What notion of distributive justice is Nussbaum advocating, then? With some of the capabilities on the list, Nussbaum argues that the objective is equal capability, such as the capability of exerting control over one's political surroundings, which is to say, equal fundamental political and civil rights for every citizen. For others, it is the threshold, or sufficient capability, that represents the societal goal. It would seem that in the case of distribution of economic resources Nussbaum regards relatively large inequalities as legitimate, so long as all citizens have access to a

---

[16] Nussbaum, *Women and Human Development*, pp. 87ff.
[17] Nussbaum, *Women and Human Development*, pp. 84ff.

certain fundamental level of social and economic security, fundamental political freedoms and rights are guaranteed, and all children enjoy equal access to education.[18] As regards the equal distribution of resources, then, it would seem as though Nussbaum is advocating a so-called sufficientarianism by which the goal of redistribution should be that everyone has sufficient resources in order to have the possibility of developing fundamental functions. Yet her line of argument can also be interpreted as presupposing a model of equal opportunities—the idea that distribution will result in a "level playing field".[19] Nussbaum additionally describes the concept of capability as a limited, or partial, understanding of social justice; it is a necessary but not sufficient condition for justice: the concept of capability establishes a lower threshold but otherwise leaves open the question of distribution.[20]

We find here a connection to how human rights are often presented, namely as precisely such a fundamental protection of human dignity, based on the idea that certain needs are so fundamental that they must be realized to a particular extent for all people. Nussbaum herself discusses what she sees as the similarities and differences between her model and human rights. One point of overlap, as she sees it, is that the list should be understood as a set of principles that can provide the basis for guarantees, enshrined in a country's constitution or bill of rights, as to the right of all people to certain minimal levels of social and political recognition by the holders of political power.[21] She further contends that the capabilities included on the list correspond to what are sometimes referred to as different generations of rights—political and civil rights as well as economic and social rights—and that the list should therefore be seen as a variant of a

[18] Nussbaum, *Frontiers of Justice,* pp. 291ff.

[19] Nussbaum, *Frontiers of Justice*, p. 292.

[20] Nussbaum, *Women and Human Development*, p. 75, *Frontiers of Justice*, p. 71.

[21] Nussbaum, *Women and Human Development*, p. 97.

theory of fundamental rights that is applicable both nationally and globally.[22]

Nussbaum enters into the classic discussion about how we should understand the function of rights. She argues that one obvious advantage to the capabilities approach is that it makes clear that the state needs to provide different kinds of guarantees and supportive systems if human beings are to be able to function in certain core ways. The classical political freedoms and rights count for little, she contends, if people are deprived of the economic and social preconditions necessary for the exercise of the functions which those rights are intended to protect in actual situations. We recognize her argument that the focus on capabilities takes its point of departure in the idea that some interaction between inner and outer conditions is necessary in order for people to be able to function within certain key areas of life. Freedom requires material support, and, just as rights become "useless" if they are not implemented by political and social institutions, so, too, must capabilities be transformed into real opportunities for functioning for every member of society.[23]

Although Nussbaum here makes an important point, my view is that she insufficiently articulates one aspect of human rights, namely the idea that the primary function of human rights is to safeguard people's fundamental (moral) right to participate in the determination of the norms to which they themselves are subject. That is to say, human rights are a matter of structures for legitimation whereby no-one should be subjected to power, norms, or institutions whose development they have had no opportunity to affect by means of (equal) rights to participation in public decision-making processes.[24] Admittedly, Nussbaum includes on her list the capability of control over one's political surroundings, by which every individual should have the oppor-

[22] Nussbaum, *Frontiers of Justice*, pp. 284f.

[23] Nussbaum, *Frontiers of Justice*, p. 287.

[24] For instance, Rainer Forst, *Justification and Critique: Towards a Critical Theory of Politics* (Cambridge, UK: Polity Press, 2014) pp. 39, 46.

tunity to take part in the governance of a democratic political order.[25] Yet she does not present any clear theoretical account of what can be said to constitute just institutions, something to which I will return in my concluding discussion.

A Theory of Justification

Nussbaum argues that the advantage of clearly identifying a truly human functioning that can form the basis for an understanding of social justice becomes especially apparent once it is compared with so-called contract theories or what she calls "procedurialism". The model of justification which Nussbaum advocates, and which she calls "a substantive good approach",[26] differs from the models of justification formulated by both John Rawls and Jürgen Habermas. Nussbaum contends that it is not possible to justify an understanding of justice without also saying something about what is a good, or desirable, human life. For that, she argues, we need a substantial understanding of the good, something she regards the notion of a truly human functioning as exemplifying.[27]

It should be remembered that Nussbaum sees her capabilities approach as compatible with the core tenets of political liberalism. The notion of truly human functioning which underpins her list must therefore be understood as a partial understanding of the good life, she argues, which makes agreement upon certain fundamental political principles possible while still according ample space to people's choices regarding how to pursue the good life. For this reason, argues Nussbaum, it is essential that the idea of human functioning she advocates can be shown to respect the multiplicity of understandings that are a necessary feature of pluralistic societies.

[25] See *Women and Human Development*, pp. 101ff.

[26] Nussbaum, *Women and Human Development*, pp. 165f.

[27] Nussbaum, *Women and Human Development*, pp. 148f, 165, *Frontiers of Justice*, pp. 148f.

In this way, according to Nussbaum, Rawls' notion of over-lapping consensus remains significant even within the capab-ilities approach. Rawls holds that the idea of justice must be for-mulated in a way that makes it possible for citizens to agree on it, despite their having different understandings of what constitutes a good life. This requires people with very different points of departure regarding what constitutes the good to be able to agree on a particular set of principles that should prevail in society. The justice model, or principles of justice, should therefore not be formulated upon the basis of a specific understanding of the good, since this would lead to citizens who do not share that understanding being excluded and, with it, render impossible an overlapping consensus.

Nussbaum argues that her list of core human capabilities is the result of a process according to which different understan-dings of human dignity have been tested against the notion of human functioning upon which the list is predicated.[28] In this connection, she here refers to interviews carried out with women in India, which she integrates into her text at various points.[29] Nussbaum uses these narratives to show that the capabilities included on the list find support from people in vastly different social contexts. She also cites examples from literary history, which she regards as offering grounds for the idea that truly human function is not limited to Western cultures. It is crucial, argues Nussbaum, that the list is capable of securing the ap-proval of people from different traditions and regions, and that for this reason it should be regarded as giving expression to an overlapping consensus.[30]

Nussbaum emphasizes that this aspect is important because she is concerned to devise a model of capability justice with universal validity. Nussbaum's denunciation of what she calls relativism or arguments based on relativism strongly suggests

[28] Nussbaum, *Women and Human Development*, pp. 101ff.
[29] Nussbaum, *Women and Human Development*, pp. 15ff.
[30] Nussbaum, *Women and Human Development*, pp. 44ff.

that she thinks it possible to offer a legitimation of the list that can find acceptance from people from different cultures and traditions. Nussbaum advocates a form of epistemological universalism which claims that we can conduct a rational conversation about moral issues transcending differences grounded in context and group identity. She furthermore argues that it is both wrong and reductive of other cultures to ascribe Western origins to the notion of human capability.[31]

Nussbaum herself actualizes the question of whether her list of capabilities risks turning out to be a form of cultural imperialism by which one tradition's conception of the good life is elevated to the status of universal norm. No, she replies, that danger is circumvented by the fact that the list can be changed once its contents become the object of revisions generated by discussion and dialogue. However, it may be noted that the contents of the list have remained the same since she first presented it, now almost twenty years ago.

Although Nussbaum claims that it is not her principal argument for the justification of the list, a recurring issue is whether the various points that comprise her capabilities approach should be the object of an overlapping consensus. It is on this point, precisely, that I would like to press her. Alison Jaggar notes that Nussbaum's statement that the list enjoys broad support from various traditions and worldviews has not been confirmed in a way that removes any doubt about selectivity and underrepresentation of perspectives that do not support her philosophical position. Here there is reason to criticize the way in which Nussbaum uses the Indian women's narratives. The latter are given to

---

[31] Nussbaum conducts a lengthy discussion about that which she denotes as "cultural relativism" and the ways in which its "defenders" are mistaken. Central to her arguments in this case is the idea that we can find ample support for the "fact" that people across the globe seem to value and strive for similar things. Therefore, the idea that everything is relative to culture is false and persons cannot be defined solely in terms of their cultural commitments. See section II in chapter 1 "In Defense of Universal Values", Nussbaum, *Women and Human Development*, pp. 41-49.

us only as part of Nussbaum's interpretation, their conversations being presented only in extremely brief excerpts.[32]

In conclusion, Nussbaum's model of justification is essentially a neo-Aristotelian understanding of the good life interpreted as truly human functioning, but, as she sees it, centered upon a pluralistic conception of human functioning that is able to find expression in different ways. Nussbaum argues that we cannot justify a notion of social justice without having a conception of what makes life good for human beings. Nussbaum's objection to so-called contract theories, which argue that moral legitimation should not presuppose a particular conception of the good, is that they are themselves unable to avoid making assumptions about what is valuable in human life. On this point, argues Nussbaum, her own model makes this relationship clear by taking as its starting point a substantial idea of truly human functioning instead of, as she puts it, "smuggling in such assumptions by the back door", in the form of different articulations of what constitutes human reason or our capacity for action and agency.

The Capabilities Approach—Some Critical Remarks

So, what should we say about the model of justice presented by Martha Nussbaum? What are its advantages and disadvantages? We can start by noting that this theory of justice has had a tremendous impact both within and beyond academia. A clear strength is that Nussbaum's capabilities approach—and she shares this achievement with Sen—has succeeded in presenting a clear idea of how we can understand justice in terms of development. Nussbaum has also contributed to the development of Aristotelianism within moral philosophy by means of a neo-Aristotelian interpretation of human functioning upon which she bases her own version of the capabilities approach. Her ver-

---

[32] Alison Jaggar "Reasoning About Well-Being: Nussbaum's Methods of Justifying the Capabilities", *Political Philosophy*, Vol. 14, No. 3, 2006, pp. 301–322, p. 313.

sion of the approach also contains a clear notion of justification. She has presented a thought-provoking critique of contract theory's focus upon mutual benefit and taken a clear stance in support of the view that people with reduced cognitive function should be included in a vision of social justice. Because Nussbaum holds that a model of justice must start from a clear notion of what constitutes a good life, her articulation of social justice can be linked to concrete proposals for enacting the reforms necessary in order to achieve a more just society. Similarly valuable is her firm advocacy of a model of justice that takes its starting point in a notion of what constitutes a dignified human life.

My criticisms of Nussbaum's argument also relate to these issues. In what follows I argue that Nussbaum's theory of justice is unsatisfactory, that her conception of human nature is essentialist, that the theory of justification upon which her model rests is unconvincing, and, finally, that the notion of a dignified life around which she constructs her model results in an unacceptably weak interpretation of the principle of human dignity.

I have already noted that Nussbaum's model of justice is not egalitarian. In my view this constitutes a serious weakness. As we have seen, Nussbaum claims that certain capabilities require equal distribution while others require only "sufficient" distribution. I have mentioned the fact that Nussbaum seems willing to accept a relatively large degree of economic inequality. There are grounds for challenging her on this point. What is a "sufficient" degree of distribution really, and how wide can an "acceptable" social division be? I find inadequate Nussbaum's claim that a more pressing task is to ensure that all people attain a particular level of fundamental of functioning in every area of capability on her list. It appears that a quite essential and urgent task for any model of justice is to address the issue of growing economic inequality, particularly on a global level.

This aspect is bound up with another dimension of Nussbaum's model that I regard as underdeveloped, namely the question of which institutions are necessary in order to combat oppression and domination. As I mentioned in my opening remarks, the question of how we can resist both exclusion and oppression is important for Nussbaum. She has sought to formulate a model of justice that can give answers to the question of how we can create a society in which all people are given the opportunity to function in a dignified way. While I am critical of her notion of threshold levels, one strength of her model is that it squarely addresses the issue of how to ensure that people are given genuine opportunities, by means of social and political guarantees, to function within a number of different areas of life. And yet her theory of justice is so focused upon outcomes that it insufficiently considers the issue of the structures and institutions which, in shaping society, form the basis for injustice, whether by the unequal allocation of resources or the domination and oppression of particular groups.

A further problem is that Nussbaum does not explicitly offer an account of political institutions in the shape of a model of democracy. Rainer Forst has directed a critique against Nussbaum's model, arguing that a theory of justice must also engage with the structures and institutions which constitute the fundamental legitimating structures of society.[33] This can also be related to the issue of how we should understand the function of human rights. Forst's argument, with which I agree, is that we ought primarily (albeit not solely) to understand human rights as a right to participate in the justification of societal institutions. For this reason the function of human rights cannot be reduced to merely establishing some kind of social minimum which everyone must attain; rather, their most important function is to challenge those structures which, by causing people to be treated as less than full members of society, deny them the status of equal participants in the justification discourse of society.[34] According to this line of argument, justice is primarily related to those conditions which either include or exclude people from

---

[33] Forst, *Justification and Critique*, pp. 20, 25ff, 34ff.
[34] Forst, *Justification and Critique*, pp. 39, 46.

this discourse. When citizens are viewed as both the subjects and the source of those rights, they are able to address the question of what is a reasonable or just division of resources and benefits. In this fashion human rights and democracy become closely intertwined: human rights are hereby understood not only as a *protection* of an individual's autonomy and agency, according to some particular level of material or social support, but also as a public and political *recognition* of the same.[35]

As already noted, Nussbaum's model gives an ambivalent answer to the question of whether it proceeds from an essentialist conception of human nature. While she insists that it gives only a partial account, one that is compatible with differing understandings of the good, it is unclear how, when it comes to human nature, the concept of truly human functioning really differs from Aristotelian essentialism.

As we have seen, Nussbaum argues with regard to the justification of the list that it is dependent upon the idea of truly human functioning being regarded as superior to other strategies in justifying the kind of substantial freedoms included in the list. As an articulation of what constitutes a dignified human life, she contends, the list and its (pluralistic) notion of a truly human functioning must demonstrably accord with our understandings of what constitutes human dignity. As a theory of justification, it is not "neutral" and there is an obvious argumentative circularity in how Nussbaum offers up as proof that which also forms a premise of her argument.

I remarked earlier that Nussbaum underscores what she sees as a major problem with "proceduralism" or "contract theories", namely that they try to extract too much from a set of "formal" criteria such as the idea of the social contract or an abstract notion of practical reason. We are familiar with her argument that a justice model should be based upon a clear understanding of what makes for a good human life. My view is that, even if we

---

[35] Forst, *Justification and Critique*, pp. 63ff.

concede this claim, it is unconvincing for Nussbaum to argue that the notion of human functioning, which she proposes, is already, or has any real chance of becoming the object of an overlapping consensus. I also contend that such a line of argument fails to provide a clear idea as to how we should understand diversity or lack of consensus regarding notions of dignity and justice. Nor does it provide a method by which to determine which statements best correspond to the idea of truly human functioning.

The issue of justifying this model is one point at which I find Nussbaum to be genuinely obscure. In places she seems to be referring to a form of immanent justification—we saw earlier that she regards her list as an articulation of human dignity under the conditions of modernity—from which she advances the idea of overlapping consensus and the list as a kind of political liberalism. At the same time, she returns continually to how the notion of truly human functioning is crucial for her theory. Yet the notion is not uncontroversial, and, as already noted, it is difficult to see how it can avoid being categorized as an essentialist conception of humanity, based as it is upon an (admittedly neo-) Aristotelian variant of teleology.

As already discussed, Nussbaum claims to be advocating an Aristotelian rather than a Kantian conception of human dignity. For her, dignity cannot be reduced to merely one aspect of our human nature, such as reason, but rather must proceed from a thoroughgoing description of what a good life is. Nussbaum makes a significant critique of rationalist theories of human dignity, and it is a particular merit that she emphasizes so strongly that we are beings who depend upon each other's care in order to lead a good life. And yet the concept of autonomy is insufficiently emphasized in her theory of human dignity, and the principle of human dignity is reduced to the notion of a threshold value for dignity. My own view is that autonomy should form an integral part of any theory of human dignity in which autonomy is given moral and political recognition by means of a conception of people's right to participate in the structures and institutions to which they are subject. It is this that Forst has in mind when he discusses, and defends, "the right to justification". Respect for human dignity can be formulated in terms of a fundamental moral right to justification. This means that social and political procedures and arrangements must be justified in ways that respect each person's status as an equal (and auto-nomous) moral and political subject.

Nussbaum emphasizes what we might call the "social dimen-sion" of human value: we are relational beings who rely upon each other and upon benign structures in order to be able to live well. However, I would argue that because human dignity has such a social dimension, it should be understood as a value that is both sustained and vulnerable to abuses in different social relations, and that both its protection and violation can find con-crete expression in a variety of ways.[36] This means that the inter-pretation of what is required in order to protect people's human dignity should always be open to revision by giving a hearing to new narratives or to narratives previously silenced.

---

[36] Elena Namli argues that both protection and violations of human value are contextual in the sense that each always occurs within concrete settings and relations, *Human Rights as Ethics, Politics, and Law* (Uppsala: Acta Univer-sitatis Upsaliensis, 2014), pp. 202f.

Work, Aging and Justice

Nora Hämäläinen

In the recent book *Aging Thoughtfully* Martha Nussbaum argues that a universal pension age—common in many European countries, while abolished in the US and Australia—is a central form of harmful discrimination against aging people.[1] The claim is striking in the way it attacks something that many people perceive as a pillar of the equitable northern European welfare state. I scrutinize her arguments for this, and her thoughts about social security and the right to a retirement pension, and argue that a universal right to continue at work may have complex negative consequences for the kind of welfare system that Nussbaum favors, where a broad range of human capabilities can be promoted for all citizens. I also discuss the implications of her ideas on retirement, on her thinking about liberalism and social justice, and the subtle but important differences it reveals between Nussbaum's anglophone liberalism and the Nordic social liberal welfare state. While in agreement with her idea that it is important to consider aging people in their particular situations, and that we need to rethink the situation of elderly people when growing numbers age in good health, I argue that the insistence on abolishing compulsory retirement is a faux pas with regard to

---

[1] Martha Nussbaum & Saul Levmore, *Aging Thoughtfully: Conversations about Retirement, Romance, Wrinkles, and Regret* (New York: Oxford University Press, 2017).

an optimal application of Nussbaum's own capabilities approach, at least in the Nordic setting.

Aging Thoughtfully is a collaboration between Nussbaum and her colleague Saul Levmore and contains essays by both on shared themes related to aging: work; love; the use of time; inheritance; power; social security, among other things. The essays are of varying kinds and allow Nussbaum to combine different aspects of her previous work, in an easily accessible and hands on manner: ancient philosophy; the study of narrative art; the capabilities approach, and her thinking about the limits of liberalism as well as about the roles of stigma and shame in social life.[2] My focal text here is the second half of chapter 2: Nussbaum's essay entitled "Must We Retire?: Is Mandatory Retirement a Good Idea?".

Casual in its address, the book is a discussion piece, also designed to work as a "think book" for academic readers who may want to reflect over aging and how to manage different aspects of life in their later years. Its tone is more easy-going than in the scholarly and theoretical work upon which Nussbaum's intellectual reputation as one of today's foremost philosophers has been built. This does not mean that we should not read it with the same demanding eye as her other texts. The question of retirement and pensions is one of great political relevance in most western countries with an aging population, a growing number of healthy and able people in their 70s and 80s, changing job

---

[2] For ancient philosophy see for example *The Fragility of Goodness* (Cambridge: Cambridge University Press, 1986), *The Therapy of Desire: Theory and Practice in Hellenistic Ethics* (Princeton: Princeton University Press, 1994); for the theme of narrative art, *Love's Knowledge* (Cambridge: Cambridge University Press, 1990), *Poetic Justice: The Literary Imagination and Public Life* (Boston, MA: Beacon Press, 1995); for the capabilities approach *Women and Social Development: The Capabilities Approach* (Cambridge: Cambridge University Press, 1999), *Creating Capabilities: The Human Development Approach* (Oxford: Belknap Press, 2011); for shame and stigma *Hiding from Humanity: Disgust, Shame and the Law* (Princeton, New Jersey: Princeton University Press, 2004), *From Disgust to Humanity: Sexual Orientation and Constitutional Law* (Oxford: Oxford University Press, 2010).

markets due to automation, and neo-liberal policies, which have since the 1990s halted the previous development toward more equitable welfare states in many western countries.[3] Considering the combination of Nussbaum's influence and a certain narrowness in her perspective on the issue of retirement, it seems to me that her intervention deserves being taken very seriously and being scrutinized in relation to her thinking on justice, human capabilities and how to create a society that provides opportunities for human flourishing for all its members.

Thus, I first look at her arguments against compulsory retirement. Second, I discuss a range of issues that, individually or together, speak in favor of compulsory retirement. Third, I reflect on Nussbaum's way of picturing retirement, and argue that she misrepresents the challenges involved in rethinking society to serve a population with growing numbers of healthy and able elderly people.

Nussbaum's Argument

Nussbaum argues that age is an arbitrary ground for excluding people from the job market, and that a universal retirement age discriminates against the elderly by limiting their freedom of choice, possibilities for self-realization, and full participation in the life of their society.

Even though she has often presented Finland and the other Nordic countries as model societies of equality and the realization of human capabilities, she finds these values compromised by the Finnish system of compulsory retirement. Knowing that her Finnish colleagues do not necessarily share her judgment, she airs the suspicion that this is a result of adaptive preference, comparable in kind (though not in degree) to the notoriously

---

[3] *Welfare States in Transition: National Adaptations in Global Economies*, ed. Gøsta Esping-Andersen (London: United Nations Research Institute for Social Development, 1996).

low expectations that third world women have for their own health and well-being.

> What worries me about Finland is that when you are told from the cradle that productive work ends at 65, you will believe it, and you will define your possibilities and projects around this. You will expect to go on the shelf and others will expect you to be on the shelf. Not to mention the absence of things like office space and research support, you won't get the invitations you are used to or the respectful treatment from younger colleagues.

> And you will not protest, because, in short order, you will come to see yourself as useless. One of my retired Finnish friends was happy initially, finding that she had more time to spend with her husband (also forced into retirement) and more time for the gym. Two years on however, she is ashamed to come to dinners after a visiting lecture by me, her friend. She feels she does not belong, and that she ought to say no, even when I invite her. This is a terrible form of psychological tyranny.[4]

From worry, she moves here, through anecdotal illustration to "terrible" and "tyranny". In the third part of this chapter, I will return to this picture of the initially happy retiree, who later finds herself excluded from academic participation. For now, it merely stands as an illustration of Nussbaum's problematization. Retirement reduces the elderly persons possibilities to contribute and be part of certain meaningful human contexts. Thus, we need, in her view, to acknowledge it as an injustice comparable to the discrimination against women, people of color, and people with disabilities. Like these other forms of discrimination, it is based on prejudice and not on the actual characteristics of the people involved. Thus, it is illegitimate:

> so far, most modern societies think that unequal treatment on the basis of age is not really discrimination, because of "nature." They are wrong. Age discrimination, of which compulsory retirement is a central form, is based on social stereotypes, not on

[4] Nussbaum, *Aging Thoughtfully*, p. 66.

any rational principle. And it is just as morally heinous as all the others.[5]

Nussbaum indicates that the only rational principles to be considered here are the actual capacities and desires of elderly people, many of whom would be both willing and able to continue work for a number of years after their current retirement age. Stereotypes may well be involved when employers judge older employees unfit for certain tasks. Combating prejudice concerning aging people as well as other groups is of course crucial for social justice and good management. But there are several reasons for retaining a compulsory pension age that have little to do with the actual fitness or unfitness of individual employees, and that rather derive their strength form the challenge of creating and upholding a fair and equitable society overall, where everyone is given equal chances to contribute and to receive. These are the kinds of reasons that I will discuss here, to see what kind of challenge they pose to Nussbaum's own view.

Compulsory Retirement From a System's Perspective

To judge the legitimacy of compulsory retirement we must broaden our outlook. We need to look at the question of retirement from a system's perspective, keeping in mind that different societies have different principles and infrastructures for the distribution of wealth and work. As Nussbaum has repeatedly stressed, not least in relation to her capabilities approach, any steps that are taken to improve the conditions of real people have to be based on a thorough knowledge of the social, political and material realities in which these people live. The realization of universal ideals requires particular knowledge and specific measures.

Since Nussbaum takes her warning example from Finland, I will heed this principle of contextualization by looking at some particularities of the Finnish context. The point here, however, is

---

[5] Nussbaum, *Aging Thoughtfully*, p. 67.

not the illumination of a particular system (which is, itself, in flux) but the kinds of aspects of contemporary societies that call for attention when assessing the fairness of retirement practices and legislation in a concrete setting.

First some simple data. The Finnish pension system builds on (i) a nationwide guaranteed pension, available for everyone above a certain age, and (ii) an earnings-related pension, which is earned through compulsory payments throughout one's working career. In the case of employees the employer takes out a pension insurance, withholds a sum from the salary and makes the payments. Self-employed entrepreneurs also make their own compulsory payments, although they have a greater measure of freedom to manipulate the size of their payments (with effects on the size of their retirement pension). Where Sweden, for example, has changed their pensions system to give more room for private pension saving, the Finnish system reflects a more traditional welfare state model, where the state system seeks to guarantee a sufficient pension.

Currently, the month when an employer turns 68 she becomes a pensioner, her working contract is terminated and she receives a monthly pension that reflects her previous earnings. It is also possible to choose to retire at an earlier age. Those born in 1954 or earlier can retire at 63, and for those born between 1954 and 1962 the lower retirement age rises by three months per year up to people born in 1962. Those born between 1962 and 1964 can retire at 65. The retirement age for people born 1965 or later will be tied to average life expectancy, and thus both the lower retirement age and the age of compulsory retirement will be higher than the current ones. Those who stay on until the upper retirement age are rewarded with higher pensions.[6]

Although regular employment contracts currently end at 68, the employer and employee can agree about continued employment on a fixed term basis. Thus, compulsory retirement does

[6] https://www.tyoelake.fi/en/

not necessarily mean the end of paid work, but rather new terms of employment. A growing number of people do continue with paid employments after retirement, as stand-in personnel, on part time contracts, or as external experts. In this way they can complement their pension income, contribute with their knowledge and experience, and fill their time with meaningful professional activities. A growing number of people also continue to work by selling their services as individual entrepreneurs.[7]

Despite a current trend toward more working pensioners, the removal of this semi-universal phase of transition would have far reaching consequences that need to be considered.

i) The Legitimacy of the Retirement System

In the current system the right to a sufficient pension is intimately tied to the universality of retirement, and it should not be taken for granted that these can be separated without loss. The current system builds on an ideal of equity: people work on average for about forty years, roughly between 25 and 65. Before their working careers they have access to free education and after it they are entitled to a pension. In spite of substantial pension payments throughout one's working career, the most part of the pensions of current pensioners are paid by people who are currently in working life. Thus the system requires a high degree of solidarity between generations and social groups. If differences in working life expectancies for different social and professional groups would increase substantially, the legitimacy of the system may be threatened, and would in any case need to be reconsidered.

Nussbaum argues for an abstract ideal system for the economic well-being and social inclusion of the elderly. But the different systems that constitute a welfare state are heterogeneous and do not stem from a general plan. They are often the results

---

[7] See Jari Kannisto: *Eläkkeellä ja työssä: Tilasto eläkeläisten työnteosta vuosina 2007–2016.* Eläketurvakeskuksen tilastoja 12/2017. https://www.etk.fi/julkaisu/elakkeella-ja-tyossa-tilastoraportti-elakelaisten-tyonteosta/

of different political processes, and have as a result of this different forms of legitimation. The basic level of social security—e.g. people's pensions, welfare payments, sick leaves, basic unemployment benefits, etc.—are designed to prevent destitution, not least with an eye on ensuring that people remain potentially active members of society. Income based unemployment benefits are the workers' protection against the vicissitudes of the job market and exploitation by employers. They also function as a balance in the economy, when people do not need to sell their homes or quickly take a lower level job to pay their bills. Work pension, again, derives its moral legitimation from being "earned" during one's working career, but also from the perception that people over 65 or 68 are, generally, no longer professionally in their prime, and in many cases not able to go on with their work as before.

Thus, what to Nussbaum looks like a degrading generalization and in some cases an unwarranted prejudice, is, in a country like Finland, a central part of elderly people's protection against the demands of the market and the surrounding capitalist and work centered society. If an increasing number of people continue to work full time after 68, this will indeed have implications for how people at retirement age are perceived and what is expected of them. What the exact consequences will be depends among other things on how many of these people there will be, for how long they want to work full time and how the political discussion around work and social security will develop.

ii) Pension and Life Time Income

There is little reason to doubt that abolishing compulsory retirement would favor a highly educated and well to do part of the population. People with physically demanding and monotonous jobs have limited possibilities to prolong their careers, compared to those with a long education, high income, relative freedom to plan their work routines and relatively more power in society. Nussbaum's example of the rabbi and cantor in her temple who recently both were "second career women" is endearing, but it is hardly typical for people who have spent their working years on hard badly paid labor to venture upon such paths.[8] In fact, it is also the educated and well paid who have better possibilities to a career change if they lose their jobs or due to health reasons cannot continue in their previous employment. If the abolishment of the pension age would prolong the careers of well to do employees, while less well to do retire at the current age, we will see growing differences in life-time income between different social groups. Growing income differences again affect the political conditions for maintaining a universalist welfare state, including decent pensions, because people in different strata of society no longer perceive themselves as equal beneficiaries of a range of income transfers and social services.

iii) 70–90 Year Olds as Workforce

If the compulsory retirement age is abolished, people over 68 become part of the regular workforce, although with the exception that they can choose to retire. This means that the available workforce grows. Many will probably retire in order to have time for other activities, and many will still be forced to retire between 60 and 70 due to health issues. How many choose to retire, will also depend on the level of pensions compared to salaries. If a decent pension level cannot be guaranteed, more people are likely to hang on to their jobs, even when other reasons would speak strongly in favor of retirement. If a large part of the population over 65 or 70 continues to work, this will have substantial consequences for the whole job market. I will return to this soon.

For the elderly a new status of potential workforce can have complicated consequences, not least in the form of a new vulnerability. In a society, where healthy people regardless of old age are (morally or through economic incentives) expected to work, a growing number of elderly people will be exposed to the vicissitudes of contemporary work culture, competing for project

---

[8] Nussbaum, *Aging Thoughtfully*, p. 62.

employments with younger parts of the workforce, and targeted for declining performance by their superiors. If stepping down from full time employment at a set age is difficult for some people, we should not assume that stepping down later, due to actual failures of performance, will be any easier.

iv) The Change of Work and the Debate about Citizen Income

When Nussbaum argues for the abolishment of a compulsory retirement age, she does not consider the state of the current job markets in the western world, and the economic and material consequences of more or less paid work. Her argument is focused on the individual person's freedom to choose, while also assuming that it is beneficial for society as a whole if people participate in paid labor as long as they can and want to.

But this latter point should not be taken for granted. Most OECD-countries have an unemployment rate between 5 and 10 percent or higher. In most of these countries the relatively well paid mid-level industry jobs have become fewer and there has been an increase in poorly paid service jobs, with less job security and part time contracts. In recent years we have seen a growing debate about the ongoing wave of disappearing jobs due to automation. An oft repeated vision is that the future will bring few highly paid and desirable jobs for experts, while the large majority will have to settle for poorly paid precarious employments.

A job market is never a zero-sum game and older people who continue working do not necessarily cause greater unemployment among the young. But with a structural unemployment even among educated people, the extension of the workforce is not unproblematic. The employers have a larger pool of potential employees and can use this to suppress salaries. There is also a substantial risk that young people enter the job market later, and that the unemployment rate among current 25–65-year-olds will grow, with the consequence of lower work pensions for them, when they reach retirement age.

To solve the present and future challenges of work and social security, different models for a citizen wage have been discussed. In Finland a small-scale citizen wage trial was conducted in 2017–2018, giving a group of 2 000 people 560 euros for living expenses without means testing.[9] The envisioned benefits for a citizen wage system are many: it could decrease the bureaucracy of the welfare state, give security, make it easier for people living on social security to accept temporary jobs, create a socially sustainable society, give people real possibilities to pursue other projects: dedicate more care to children and aging parents, engage in artistic projects, do volunteer work for causes they find important. This debate is of course fueled by the vision that there will be less, rather than more, paid work available in the future. For the left a sufficient citizen wage represents a path to distributing the gains of increased automation, while the people on the right see a minimal citizen wage as a source of cheap and flexible labor.

In a well-functioning citizen wage society, the transfer to retirement would not be as drastic as it is for many people today, because paid work would not be as central for people's identity as active members of society, and both young and old could hop in and out of paid jobs. But in a current increasingly precarious wage-earner society the extension of the job market to the elderly looks as though it principally benefits capital in addition to strategically weakening one of the pillars of the welfare state, the comprehensive work-pension system.

---

[9] The current trial was criticized by the left party MP Anna Kontula and party leader Li Andersson. Andersson observed that it only targeted the question of possible employment effects for the currently unemployed, while neglecting the effects of a similar arrangement for other groups. https://www.kansanuutiset.fi/artikkeli/3593396-perustulokokeilu-ei-tassa-mitaan-perustuloa-kokeilla

v) The Limits of Economic Growth

There are also environmental issues to be taken into account when we think about work. In September 2017 Finnish media saw a small scandal, when the debutant author Ossi Nyman (39) in an interview in the leading capital newspaper *Helsingin Sanomat* said that he has always tried to avoid paid work, because a majority of jobs are unnecessary and contribute to over consumption. This was of course just a ripple of a growing international debate on the connection between work hours and global warming. If debates about downshifting a few years ago were about young well to do adults who chose a simpler lifestyle and fewer working hours in exchange for more free time, this issue is now more and more considered as a collective environmental one.[10]

How work affects the environment depends on what people do for work, how they get to work and what their work spaces are like. More staff in kindergartens and more nurses in elderly care or hospitals are probably more environmentally friendly than more working hours in export companies. An academic who sits at home writing is more sustainable than one who continuously flies to conferences. Emissions from traffic and electricity can also in many cases be reduced by fewer work days per week.

If a later retirement age would lead not only to a larger potential workforce, but also to more hours on the job, increased production of goods, and more travel, this would have consequences for the environment that should not be neglected.

vi) Power and its Distribution

Another issue that we need to address is the question of power. Compulsory retirement from full time positions guarantees a rotation of people in different positions of power: in businesses,

[10] For discussion see for example Andy Becket, "Post-Work: The Radical Idea of a World without Jobs", *The Guardian* January 18, 2018; Alex Williams, "Why Three-Day Weekends could help to Save the World", *The Independent*, August 29, 2016.

138

government bodies, local administration, universities and expert bodies. Retirement mostly means the loss of previous power: from boss to potential external expert, from professor in charge of a research group to an emeritus without funding. Compulsory retirement guarantees that this rotation happens at a reasonable and predictable rate. We also avoid situations where people with great power and ailing abilities stick to their position much longer than what is beneficial for the whole organization. Ideally the rotation of power supports a working culture where power is not considered a personal entitlement, but a series of tasks that one takes up and is ready to pass on after a certain time.

Nussbaum's discussion of the aging academic is particularly problematic from this point of view, reflecting perhaps too much of her own emotions with regard to retirement. Expressing relief over the fact that as an American she does not need to retire, and focusing on the indignity of losing power, office spaces and research assistants, she seems to suggest that such gained privileges are indispensable for a flourishing life of the aging academic. We could turn the question around and ask: why does she think that some people should be able to keep their power and privileges until they no longer manage to use them, rather than give them up at a fixed time so that others can hold them in turn, and move on to other roles in relation to the research community or society at large.

In academia a pool of active emeriti in fact extends the human resources of many disciplines in ways which would be difficult to replace. Especially in a small country, where academic posts in any discipline are scarce, the prospect of retirements and rotation is also crucial for attracting gifted young people to an academic career.

Nussbaum seems at a system's level to endorse the idea that it is beneficial for society if people extend their working careers. This is a vision that has for a long time been accepted by right wing and social democratic parties alike, all of whom are concerned with a sufficient influx of tax money to keep the public sector going, without having e.g. to redirect taxes towards ownership.

But there are, as we have seen, several reasons to question this idea, if one is interested in creating and upholding a more sustainable and equitable welfare state. With an eye on social welfare in a changing society it is important to distribute work more evenly between individuals, and not to increase differences in lifetime income unnecessarily. Moreover, with the other eye on global warming it is time to reconsider our life style and infrastructures, in ways which may necessitate a decrease of paid labor.

This is not to say that such considerations override the individual person's moral claim to an active participatory role in society. The question is rather how we can balance the claims of a new category of increasingly healthy and active elderly people with the above kinds of considerations and risks.

A Second Glance at the Terrible Retirement

In a sympathetic and humorous Q&A interview with the *Guardian* in 2007, Nussbaum candidly expresses her fear of dying.

> What is your greatest fear?
>
> Dying.
>
> (…)
>
> What would your super power be?
>
> Immortality.[11]

This would of course be of little philosophical interest were it not for the fact that the spirit of these answers is very much present in her writing about aging. Stepping down, giving up, retiring, are all preparations for the fact that, regardless of our current health, we will one day no longer be here. This is bound to be extremely uncomfortable for anyone attracted by the idea of immortality. While we need to age thoughtfully, this does not for

---

[11] Martha Nussbaum, Q&A Martha Nussbaum, Interview by Rosanna Greenstreet, *The Guardian*, Saturday 27 October 2007.

Nussbaum mean we should give up on our worldly ambitions and the desire to conquer new areas of life and excellence, on equal terms with younger people.

I think most of us, regardless of age, are charmed by people who manage to carry on with energy and vitality into their 70s, 80s and even their 90s, and see such people as natural role-models. But the desire and capacity to live fully to the end can be channeled in different ways, and it is not an unquestionable benefit, if given free range on the job market.

In the previous section I have placed the question of retirement age in concrete structures of work and welfare, to show that political decisions concerning retirement have complicated and potentially problematic implications for a functioning welfare society and an equitable distribution of income. Looking at this from Nussbaum's point of view, such implications are mere blips in a contingent and imperfect system, and should be given no authority in determining what society should be like.

Designing a utopian society from scratch, I would perhaps be inclined to agree with her that we need to reconsider the need for a retirement age. But in any society with a structural conflict concerning the price of labor between workforce and capital, and where social transfers of income are the product of political struggles rather than a beneficent mastermind, we need to proceed cautiously. In the current situation, giving up on a fixed retirement age would be a gain for the capital and for a limited number of relatively well-off senior workers.

The question is, do we need to nudge the Nordic welfare model in the direction of the relative social insecurity of the American scene, just to allow some people over 68 to flourish professionally? Or, in other words, does compulsory retirement really infringe elderly people's access to a meaningful and active life in a way that would motivate a system shift, even if this shift is deemed to increase social and economic vulnerability? And do we have reason to agree that compulsory retirement is an injustice from the point of view of human capabilities? Perhaps not.

We should ask why Nussbaum gives so much room to the individual person's entitlement to work. Part of the answer has to do with the work centeredness of contemporary western middle-class life style. The contemporary ideal citizen is a wage earner or an entrepreneur, whose work is her passion and who does not count working hours. A large part of the important things in our lives happen on the job, and many of our most important human relationships are work related. The leisured gentleman of the 19th and early 20th centuries disappeared with the second world war and housewives have lost ground with feminism and the entrance of middle-class women into the job market in the 60's and 70's. Even the extremely wealthy are often represented in media as hardworking, in their chosen line of employment. Love and work are the cornerstones of our humanness, as the oft repeated "quote", popularly attributed to Sigmund Freud, puts it.[12] Our current social imaginary does not furnish us with sufficient models for a flourishing life without work, and there seems to us to be something irretrievably lacking in many other kinds of worthwhile activities, when compared to paid work. Nothing quite lives up to the combination of fulfillment, usefulness and social legitimacy associated with it. Under such conditions the transition to retirement is likely to be followed by a sense of uselessness.

But to know what Nussbaum's demands are worth we need to look closer at her view of what it is like to be retired. She argues that compulsory retirement places people outside active society, making them unnecessary, incapable of contributing and secluded from contacts with younger people outside the context of the family. But she gives a very narrow if not quite misleading picture of what it means to be retired in a country with a compulsory retirement age. As noted before, at least in Finland and

---

[12] One source of this popular attribution may be Erik H. Eriksson who in *Childhood and Society* (New York: W.W. Norton & Company, 1964), p. 265 writes: "Freud, in the curt way of his old days, is reported to have said *'Lieben und Arbeiten'*."

Sweden retirement does not mean the end of paid work, and part time arrangements after retirement are increasingly common. Swedish and Finnish pensioners are frequently active in NGOs and societies with mixed age structures: they do voluntary work of different kinds; they are politically active; they write books and articles, and keep cultural institutions going by making up a large part of the audience of theaters, classical concerts and public talks. The younger pensioners have a central role in providing care and companionship for grandchildren and, increasingly, for their own aging parents in their last declining years.

The retired friend in Nussbaum's anecdote, who no longer feels welcome at academic events, may be quite real, but her experience, as rendered by Nussbaum, is not representative of the position that emeriti have in Finnish academia. Especially in those disciplines where research can be pursued without costly equipment, many people go on writing and teaching, and are active and frequent participants at seminars and conferences. I do not doubt that relinquishing a position as a central node in the teaching and research of a department may be difficult for those who have enjoyed that role. But the difficulties of negotiating a new role should not be confused with exclusion. Surely much can be done for a more systematic and organized inclusion of emeriti in academic activities, as well as for the use of retired people's knowledge and capacities in other fields. But inclusion does not have to mean the maintenance of previous power and privileges.

Nussbaum's fixation on paid labor as central for elderly people's social belonging speaks volumes about not only a contemporary society where other forms of participation are looked down upon, but also Nussbaum's own derogatory view about these other forms. This is why the loss of a salary, a position in the workplace hierarchy and professional recognition appear overwhelming and debilitating. In a sense she is right to claim that these losses decrease the pensioners' capabilities, insofar as they put limits on what these people can do or be in their societies, that is, what kinds of prestige and power they can hold and where they can continue to make themselves necessary. But given that we may be facing a decline in the demand for paid work, it would make more sense to re-imagine belonging, recognition and purposeful activity instead. How should we tap the resources of emeriti, to the benefit of the academic community? How can we facilitate the transition from paid work to other activities? Perhaps we need to reimagine working life itself, to make room for a plurality of engagements during people's working years. These kinds of measures would also be beneficial for the realization of the various capabilities of those who find themselves outside the workforce in their youth or middle years, due to unemployment, caring duties, illness or the like.

For an average Nordic academic, Nussbaum's political and social thought tends to appear strikingly uncontroversial. The kinds of positive rights and entitlements to education, health, recreational activities and culture for which she has argued as necessities for human flourishing, have for decades been taken for granted in the Nordic countries as a basis for a civilized society. Often political struggles have been about *what* and *how much*, but there has been a firm consensus over the beneficial effects of the welfare state across political boundaries. In more recent years, under the pressure of neo-liberal politics and in the aftermath of the economic crises of the 1990s and 2000s some aspects of the welfare state, such as equal and affordable elderly care, have dwindled. At least Finns and Swedes have learned a kind of double think: most people still consider such entitlements to be fundamental and believe that they are in place as before, even after systematic cuts have been made, making them much less available. In this situation of system shift or decline, Nussbaum's defense of basic capabilities has offered a renewed theoretical framework for thinking about the public sector and its services, and has made her a popular speaker as well as a useful reference point for ongoing public policy debates.

Nussbaum's argument against compulsory retirement reveals, however, an important point where her own thought and the ethos of the Nordic welfare state differ. For her, individual freedom and entitlement takes precedence over equity and holistic governance of work and income, to the extent that the reasons for a compulsory retirement age (many of which are obvious to quite ordinary citizens of a Nordic welfare state) become no reasons at all.

In her book *Frontiers of Justice* Nussbaum argues that the liberal contractualist tradition needs to be extended by accommodating initial differences in people's capacities to participate in the bargaining over what a just society would be like.[13] Focusing on the rights of women, people with disabilities and non-human animals, she argues that the liberal social contract tradition fails to cover their moral entitlements due to an incapacity to adequately represent their moral claims. Now she states that "compulsory retirement, the leading form of age discrimination, is one of the great moral evils of our times, the next frontier of justice that any theory of justice must address".[14] It is timely to talk about aging as the next frontier of justice, especially if we look at the state of elderly care even in many parts of the affluent world, but it is a mistake to make compulsory retirement a central target. The idea that equal terms of employment into old age would be a fundamental right, does not go very well with Nussbaum's larger thinking about justice and social security. Instead of a new freedom, we risk fueling the present capitalist logic, to the detriment of both old and young. The right to work easily turns into a moral duty and economic necessity to make oneself available on the job market as long as one can. The healthy and active years after retirement, which are now available for a substantial part of the retiring generation, might in the future be a privilege of those few who can retire early on private means, while a large majority once again wear themselves out at work.

I have here mainly criticized Nussbaum's view because of the way it is likely to clash with the crass realities of current economy and political thinking. In her defense we could ask: should

---

[13] Nussbaum, *Frontiers of Justice* (Boston: Harvard University Press, 2006).
[14] Nussbaum, *Aging Thoughtfully*, p. 68.

we not be able to maintain a more utopian outlook, and look for means to its realization? But the crucial question is which combination of realism and utopianism we are willing to opt for. Rather than imagining a society where everyone regardless of age can be sucked into a predominantly capitalist job market according to individual desires, talents and capacities, I would like to see a society which can formulate a coherent defense of people and their worthwhile pursuits, against the vicissitudes of the market. My utopia would be a citizen society where opportunities to paid work and social benefits are distributed in both fair and equal ways, leaving sufficient room for self-realization and meaningful activities outside work. In some possible future we may give up the universal retirement age as an unnecessary limitation to people's individual liberty, but that future is not here yet.

Authors

Anders Burman is professor of Intellectual History at Södertörn University. Three of his main areas of research are the history of educational ideas, the tradition of Hegelian Marxism, and Hannah Arendt's thinking. He has written, edited or co-edited around thirty books, among them the monographs *Flykten från Hegel: Den postmoderna vänsterns genealogi* (2016) and *Kultiverandet av det mänskliga: Essäer om liberal education, bildning och tänkande* (2018) as well as the anthologies *Att läsa Arendt* (2017) and *Hegelian Marxism: The Uses of Hegel's Philosophy in Marxist Theory from Georg Lukács to Slavoj Žižek* (with Anders Bartonek, 2018).

Jenny Ehnberg is researcher at the Church of Sweden Research Department. Her research field is theological ethics with a focus on questions relating to political ethics, democracy, human rights, global ethics and justice. Publications include, *Communication, and Justice: A Critical Study of Global Ethics* (2015) and recently an anthology on the role of theology in society entitled: *Forskning i skärningspunkten mellan akademi, samhälle och kyrka* (2019).

Nora Hämäläinen is senior researcher at the Centre for Ethics as Study in Human Value, University of Pardubice, Czech Republic. She is author of *Literature and Moral Theory* (2015, paperback 2017) and *Descriptive Ethics: What does Moral Philosophy Know about Morality* (2016), and *Är Trump postmodern?: En essä om sanning och populism* (2019). She has also recently co-edited *Reading Iris Murdoch's Metaphysics as a Guide to Morals* (with Gillian Dooley, 2019).

Synne Myrebøe is an assistant professor at Södertörn University. Her main research-interests are intellectual history within the fields of feminist, pedagogical and political philosophy. She defended her thesis *Kultiveringens politik: Martha Nussbaum, antiken och filosofins praktik* in May 2019.

Mats Persson is professor of History of Ideas and Science at Uppsala University. His current research interests concerns the theory and history of historical thinking, and ancient philosophy. Among recent articles are "In the Midst of Demons: Eros and Temporality in Plato's Symposium", in Ingela Nilsson (ed.), *Plotting with Eros: Essays on the Poetics of Love and the Erotics of Reading* (with Dimitrios Iordanoglou, 2009), "Tidigare än, men ändå samtida: Det förflutna i antik grekisk historieskrivning", *Lychnos* 2012 (with Dimitrios Iordanoglou) and "Platonsk kärlek I–III", *Arche: Tidskrift för psykoanalys, humaniora och arkitektur* 2016–2017.

Sharon Rider is professor of Philosophy at Uppsala University. She is currently Deputy Director of *Engaging Vulnerability* and her work focuses on the cultural conditions for autonomy, responsibility and knowledge, and how these might be conceptualized in ways that neither reject nor rely on conventional notions of rational agency. Her publications include *Post-truth, Fake News: Viral Modernity and Higher Education* (2018) and "Coercion by Necessity or Comprehensive Responsibility? Hannah Arendt on Vulnerability, Freedom and Education", in Véronique Fóti & Pavlos Kontos (eds.), *Phenomenology and the Primacy of the Political* (2017).

Charlotta Weigelt is professor of Philosophy at the School of Culture and Education, Södertörn University. Her main research interests are ancient philosophy and phenomenology, with a particular focus on questions pertaining to the philosophy of science and knowledge. Among her most recent publications are: "'The Soul is in a Way All Things': Aristotle and Internalist Conceptions of Intentionality", *Aristotle on Logic and Nature*, ed. Jan-Ivar Lindén (2019), "The Political Implications of Dialectic in Plato and Aristotle: The Question of Ruling", *Eranos* No. 109, 2018, and "Aristotelian Dialectic as Midwifery: The Epistemic Significance of Critique", *Bochumer Philosophisches Jahrbuch für Antike und Mittelalter* 20, 2017.

Martha Nussbaum's Books

Aristotle's De Motu Animalium
(Princeton: Princeton University Press, 1978).

The Fragility of Goodness: Luck and Ethics in Greek Tragedy and Philosophy (Cambridge: Cambridge University Press, 1986).

Love's Knowledge: Essays on Philosophy and Literature
(New York: Oxford University Press, 1990).

The Therapy of Desire: Theory and Practice in Hellenistic Ethics
(Princeton: Princeton University Press, 1994).

Poetic Justice: The Literary Imagination and Public Life
(Boston: Beacon Press, 1995).

For Love of Country: A Debate on Patriotism and Cosmopolitanism
(Boston: Beacon Press, 1996).

Cultivating Humanity: A Classical Defense of Reform in Liberal Education (Cambridge: Harvard University Press, 1997).

Sex and Social Justice
(New York: Oxford University Press, 1999).

Women and Human Development: The Capabilities Approach
(New York: Cambridge University Press, 2000).

Upheavals of Thought: The Intelligence of Emotions
(Cambridge: Cambridge University Press, 2001).

Hiding From Humanity: Disgust, Shame, and the Law
(Princeton: Princeton University Press, 2004).

Frontiers of Justice: Disability, Nationality, Species Membership
(Cambridge: Harvard University Press, 2006).

The Clash Within: Democracy, Religious Violence, and India's Future (Cambridge: Harvard University Press, 2007).

Liberty of Conscience: In Defense of America's Tradition of Religious Equality (New York: Basic Books, 2008).

The Ethics and Politics of Compassion and Capabilities, with Joseph Chan, Joe Lau, and Ci Jiwei (Hong Kong: Faculty of Law, 2007).

From Disgust to Humanity: Sexual Orientation and Constitutional Law (New York: Oxford University Press, 2010).

Not For Profit: Why Democracy Needs the Humanities (Princeton: Princeton University Press, 2010).

Seneca, Anger, Mercy, Revenge. In The Complete Works of Lucius Annaeus Seneca, edited by Elizabeth Asmis, Shadi Bartsch, and Martha Nussbaum (Chicago: The University of Chicago Press, 2010).

Creating Capabilities: The Human Development Approach (Cambridge: Harvard University Press, 2011).

Philosophical Interventions: Reviews 1986–2011 (Oxford: Oxford University Press, 2012).

The New Religious Intolerance: Overcoming the Politics of Fear in an Anxious Age (Cambridge: Harvard University Press, 2012).

Political Emotions: Why Love Matters For Justice (Cambridge: Harvard University Press, 2013).

Anger and Forgiveness (New York: Oxford University Press, 2016).

Aging Thoughtfully, with Saul Levmore (New York: Oxford University Press, 2017).

The Monarchy of Fear: A Philosopher Looks at Our Political Crisis (New York: Simon and Schuster, 2018).

The Cosmopolitan Tradition: A Noble but Flawed Ideal (Cambridge: Belknap Harvard, 2019).

Index

Södertörn Studies in Intellectual and Cultural History

www.ingramcontent.com/pod-product-compliance
Lightning Source LLC
Chambersburg PA
CBHW030838090426
42737CB00009B/1014